If **DINOSAURS** were **ALIVE** **TODAY**

Author
Dougal Dixon

Consultant
Professor Mike Benton
University of Bristol

9 8 7 6 5 4 3 2 1
Digit on the right indicates the number of this printing

ISBN-10: 0-7624-3329-9

Printed in China

With special thanks to our team of illustrators: *Leonello Calvetti, Frank DeNota, Andrew Kerr,*
Simon Mendez, Peter Scott, Franco Tempesta

ticktock Project Manager: *Jo Hanks*
ticktock Project Designer: *Graham Rich*
US Project Editor: *T.L. Bonaddio*
Designers: *Matt Harding, James Powell, Lee Playle, Justin Spain*
Picture Research: *Julia Adams, Jo Hanks, Lizzie Knowles*

Additional thanks to: *Becca Clunes, Sophie Furse*
Consultant: *Professor Mike Benton, University of Bristol*

This book may be ordered by mail from the publisher. Please include $2.50 for postage and handling.
But try your bookstore first!

This edition published by **Running Press Kids**, an imprint of
Running Press Book Publishers
2300 Chestnut Street
Philadelphia, PA 19103-4371
Visit us on the web!
www.runningpress.com

THE STORY OF THE DINOSAURS

Planet Earth is around 4.5 billion years old. Rocks containing traces of living things show us that **there has been life on Earth for around 3.6 billion years.** During Earth's long history, living things have been constantly changing shape and structure.

Most of the earliest organisms on Earth cannot be traced. This is because they were soft-bodied, and disintegrated when they died. But then, about **500 million years ago, creatures with hard shells appeared.** The shells of these animals could be fossilized. So when they died, **they left behind fossils preserved in rocks.** The development of animals with hard shells was one of the most significant events in the history of life on our planet.

The next important event in Earth's history was when **the earliest life-forms** left the oceans and **began to colonize the land, 400 million years ago.** Once life on land became established, **Earth's animals began to diversify and develop** in many different directions.

The dinosaurs were the most famous and fascinating group of animals from these prehistoric times. **Dinosaurs were the biggest land-living creatures that have ever lived.** Alongside these giants lived smaller, bird-like dinosaurs, massive flying reptiles and gargantuan, ocean-dwelling monsters.

Then, 65 million years ago, the dinosaurs were suddenly gone. Scientists still do not know for sure what ended the Age of Dinosaurs. A giant asteroid may well have been the main cause, wiping out most living things. The sudden extinction of the dinosaurs left Earth open for colonization by a new group of animals. **It was the rise of the mammals.** The most recent development in the existence of mammals took place **less than 4 million years ago** when *Homo sapiens*, humans, appeared!

Homo sapiens were different from the mammals that had gone before. **They were intelligent,** with an ability to use tools and form social cultures. Even from these earliest times, humans wondered about the history of their planet and **they questioned the existence of life on Earth.**

Mankind began observing rocks and the fossils they contained, and built up stories about them. Huge fossilized bones were thought to be from giants and dragons that lived long before people. Tales of these mythical animals were told in cultures around the world. But in the 18th century, a few people realized that fossils were the remains of plants and animals that had existed before humans.

By the 1800s, fossil hunting was a popular pastime and the science of palaeontology, (studying fossil animals and plants), was born. In 1842, the English scientist Sir Richard Owen invented the term "Dinosauria" to describe the giant creatures that had once walked the Earth. Their remains began to arouse the curiosity of both scientists and ordinary people.

For over two centuries, dinosaurs have amazed and fascinated us. We wonder how dinosaurs would compare to the familiar animals of our world today. How vast would a towering *Sauroposeidon* seem alongside today's biggest land-living animal, the African elephant? Could these ancient herbivores actually survive today? In today's landscapes, eating today's plants, in competition with today's animals?

And what about the ferocious and massive prehistoric meat-eaters? Could their hunting styles adapt to the prey that is available today? Could *Tyrannosaurus* catch an antelope? Could any prehistoric hunter outrun today's fastest predator — the cheetah? Is it possible that prehistoric, ocean predators were big enough to attack and kill modern-day whales?

We may never have the chance to see these animals as they were. All we can do at the moment is imagine them. We can take what we have discovered about them from their fossilized remains, and compare it with what we know about modern animals.

But imagine if we could see these amazing creatures from history, in action. Imagine if we could study them, touch them, and walk amongst them. How awe-inspiring and how terrifying would it be to live alongside these giants? Could we control them? How would our landscape and our cities look? What wonders would the seas and skies hold?

What would life be like......... If Dinosaurs Were Alive Today?

Giants of the Plains

The hot sun beats down on the burning, dry plains. A herd of elephants gather at a watering hole to drink and bathe. Each of the giant mammals weighs the same as 50 men and stands at over 11.5 feet tall. They push and splash, enjoying the cooling water. Suddenly a monstrous creature, that dwarfs even the largest elephant in the herd, towers over them. A huge *Sauroposeidon* is wading into the shallow water. Twice as tall at the shoulder and ten times heavier than the biggest of the elephants, the great dinosaur moves among the tusked giants.

Sauroposeidon was the tallest animal to have ever walked on Earth. It must have dwarfed all the other animals on the open plains of the early Cretaceous world. It fed on tall trees, like the giraffe, and was a member of the brachiosaurid group of long-necked plant-eaters. The elephants move away, but are in no danger from this vast, gentle herbivore—unless it accidently knocks one of them over with its massive tail!

Sauroposeidon

Fossil finds Just four huge neck vertebrae have been found at the Antlers Rock Formation, in Oklahoma, USA.

Name *Sauroposeidon* meaning "lizard of Poseidon" (the ancient Greek earthquake god).

Time Early Cretaceous period, 112 million years ago.

Classification Macronians—the "big noses." They belonged to the group known as brachiosaurids—these were amongst the biggest prehistoric land-living animals known.

Habitat Open plains with some woodland.

Physical Characteristics They belonged to the sauropod (lizard-footed) dinosaurs—the group of plant-eaters with long necks.

DINOSAUR DESIGN

When the neck vertebrae of *Sauroposeidon* were first found, palaeontologists thought that they were fossilized tree trunks because the fossils were so big!

The neck vertebrae were thin and light with a honeycomb arrangement of air cavities. This made the neck lighter and easier to lift.

Fossilized tree trunk
(cross section)

Sauroposeidon
neck vertebra (cross section)

Bone

Bone cavity

DINOSAUR DETECTIVES

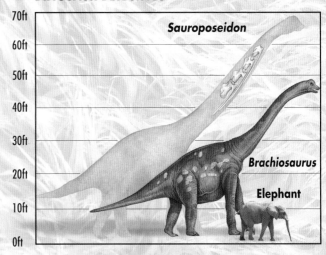

70ft
60ft
50ft
40ft
30ft
20ft
10ft
0ft

Sauroposeidon

Brachiosaurus

Elephant

Palaeontologists used the dimensions and shapes of *Brachiosaurus* neck bones to work out that *Sauroposeidon* was an animal that looked very much like *Brachiosaurus*, but was much, much bigger.

Battering Ram

A loud crack echoes around a snowy valley in the Rocky Mountains. It sounds like a gunshot but it is actually the noise of two skulls crashing together. A Bighorn ram and a *Stegoceras* are clashing. It is mating season for the rams. They resent intruders, fighting off any animal they see as competition. Sit tight, this butting contest could last for twenty hours!

Stegoceras would probably be at home in the mountainous areas of today's world. It was well-equipped to deal with hardy mountain animals. *Stegoceras* was built like a battering ram. Solid bones at the top of its head absorbed the impact when it collided with a rival—preventing it from damaging itself. A very strong neck and back stopped the animal's body from twisting when fighting, making it an incredibly strong dinosaur.

Stegoceras

Fossil finds Montana, USA; Alberta, Canada.

Name *Stegoceras*, meaning "roof-horn."

Time Late Cretaceous period, 83 — 70 million years ago.

Classification
Marginocephalians—the dinosaurs with ornamentation on their heads. The pachycephalosaurids, the group of marginocephalians to which *Stegoceras* belonged, were those with a bony dome on top of their skulls.

Habitat Possibly upland areas.

Physical characteristics
Small two-footed dinosaur, with a solid skull.

BONEHEAD

Stegoceras was a member of the pachycephalosaurids—the "thick-headed lizards." They are so-called because of the massive dome of bone on the top of their skull. This was probably used as a battering ram; for head-butting their rivals when competing for leadership of the herd, or for defending the herd from predators.

They may have butted one another on the flanks, as well as head-to-head.

FIGHT OR FLIGHT?

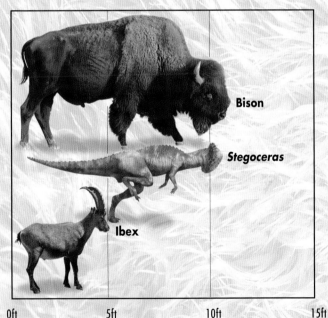

Bison

Stegoceras

Ibex

0ft   5ft   10ft   15ft

All pachycephalosaurs had thick, domed skulls which they used to protect themselves. However, scientists think they also had a good sense of smell, alerting them to predators in time to run away.

Keeping Cool

An exhausted camel rests in the shade of an *Ouranosaurus'* sail. It's June and temperatures in Egypt have soared to 41°C (100°F). There are not many places to cool down in. It is not a problem for *Ouranosaurus* because of its sail. Supported by long spines and filled with blood vessels, the sail can be held into the wind to cool the animal's circulating blood.

Some scientists think that the spines on *Ouranosaurus'* back supported a fatty hump rather than a sail. The lump would have been like that of a camel, and used as a source of nutrition when conditions were really harsh. With the increase in global warming, animals with exotic heat regulating devices, like *Ouranosaurus*, might do well.

Ouranosaurus

Fossil finds Niger, Africa.

Name *Ouranosaurus*, meaning "brave monitor lizard."

Time Early Cretaceous period, 125 — 112 million years ago.

Classification Ornithopods—plant-eating dinosaurs with bird-like feet. Most were small and two-footed, but the bigger ones walked on all fours. The iguanodontids were fairly primitive members of this group, and *Ouranosaurus* was one of these.

Habitat Open scrubland.

Physical characteristics Large iguanodontid with a spectacular sail down its back and tail.

A PROMINENT FEATURE

The sail of *Ouranosaurus* was supported by a series of long, broad spines down the backbone, arranged like a picket fence. It was not unique. The big meat-eater *Spinosaurus*, that lived at the same time in the same area, had a similar structure. It may have been used for warming and cooling the body, or it may have supported a fatty hump like a camel's for food storage during lean seasons.

HOT OR COLD—NO PROBLEM!

Ouranosaurus

Blue Rock Lizard

Ouranosurus' sail helped it to regulate its body temperature. In the same way, this modern-day lizard has flattened its body to create a larger area through which it absorbs heat from the rock.

Under Attack

A white rhinoceros feels the ground shuddering beneath its feet and senses danger. The rhinoceros' instincts are right. At three tons, the adult *Styracosaurus* that has blundered into its path is a formidable opponent. But the rhinoceros is a fierce rival—weighs the same and is desperate to protect its territory. It starts to charge. Six tons of muscles are about to collide.

Back in late Cretaceous times, herds of *Styracosaurus* shared their habitat with herds of other horned dinosaurs. They could recognize one another by the arrangements of horns and other head ornamentation, so the different species of ceratopsians could keep to their own territories. The different horn arrangement of the white rhino would certainly signal to *Styracosaurus* that this is a different animal—to be avoided or challenged.

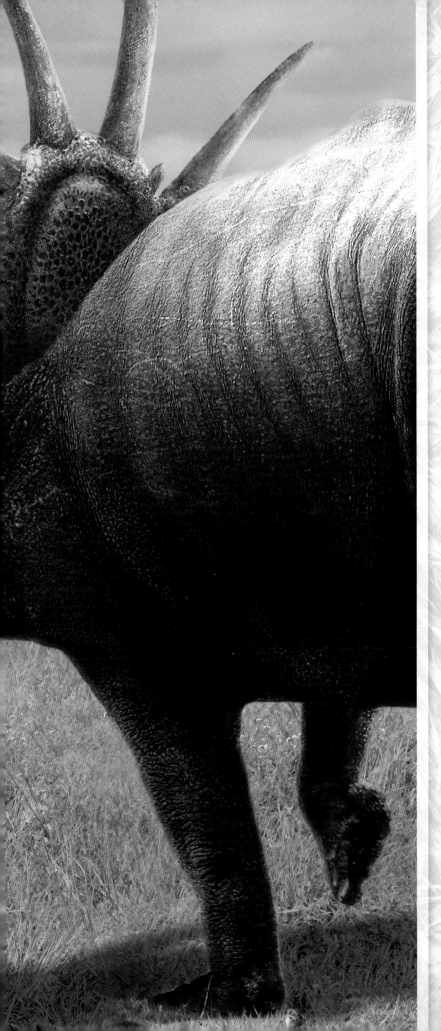

Styracosaurus

Fossil finds Montana, USA; Alberta, Canada.

Name *Styracosaurus*, meaning "spiked lizard."

Time Cretaceous period, 135 — 65 million years ago.

Classification
Marginocephalians—dinosaurs with head ornaments. Within this group the ceratopsians were the horned dinosaurs, with armored shields around the neck and horns on the face.

Habitat Open woodland.

Physical characteristics
A short-frilled ceratopsian with a long nose horn and horns around the edge of the neck frill.

FRILLY HEAD

Styracosaurus' enormous head frills and horn made it look much bigger and scarier than it actually was. Their purpose was to scare predators away. Scientists think that the dinosaur was probably brightly colored, again to frighten away attackers.

LONG AND SHORT HORNS

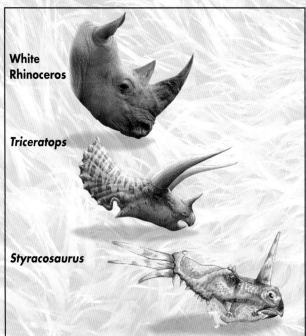

White Rhinoceros

Triceratops

Styracosaurus

Triceratops and *Styracosaurus* had different arrangements of horns on their heads—just like a modern rhinoceros. Different species were distinguished by the number of horns they had.

13

Boxing Bout

Out of the thickets comes a young *Plateosaurus*, reaching around for twigs and needles on the forest floor. Suddenly it is attacked by a tiger—such a big animal would be a tempting meal to the modern meat-eater. The *Plateosaurus* isn't as slow as its bulk might suggest, it whips its tail around and knocks the tiger off its feet.

Plateosaurus was well-used to the sparse vegetation of the Triassic landscape. In *Plateosaurus'* own time the meat-eaters were small but active theropods. Despite the big claw on its forefeet, it would not be well equipped to defend itself against the main meat-eaters of today.

Plateosaurus

Fossil finds Germany; Switzerland and France.

Name *Plateosaurus*, meaning "broad lizard."

Time Late Triassic period, 225 – 200 million years ago.

Classification Prosauropods—the earliest of the long-necked plant-eaters. They had big bodies, and could walk either on their hind legs or on all fours. One family gave rise to the later sauropods—the really big, long-necked plant-eating dinosaurs.

Habitat Desert oases.

Physical characteristics Large heavy-bodied prosauropod.

THE FIRST OF ITS KIND

Plateosaurus was the first of the big plant-eating dinosaurs. It roamed northern Europe in herds, probably moving from one fertile area to another as the seasons progressed. Several fossil skeletons have been found that tell the story of a *Plateosaurus* trapped in the quicksand of a dried stream bed, and pulled to pieces by small meat-eating dinosaurs, and the crocodile-like reptiles that existed at the time.

SMART CHART

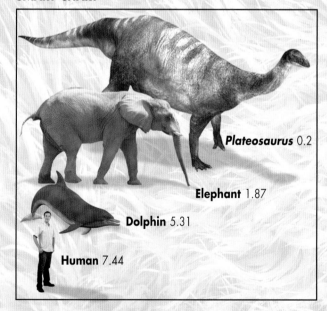

Plateosaurus 0.2

Elephant 1.87

Dolphin 5.31

Human 7.44

Scientists work out the intelligence of animals by comparing the size of their brain with the size of their body. The chart starts at zero and finishes at eight. As you can see the *Plateosaurus* is very low on the scale—in fact no modern animal comes lower than it!

Clever Decoy

Three playful sifakas spy a stranger in their thicket. They feel intrigued and a little intimidated. They throw themselves at the newcomer's head, taunting it and leaping away. But their target is not really the intruder's head—it is its tail. The big animal is a juvenile *Ankylosaurus*. For such a heavy animal, the attack of the sifakas is hardly even an annoyance. It lumbers on regardless.

Ankylosaurus was one of the armored dinosaurs that carried a heavy club on the end of its tail. As well as a weapon that could be swung like a medieval mace, the club may have acted as a decoy. The superficial resemblance to a head may have drawn an attack away from more vulnerable parts of the body. *Ankylosaurus* had huge muscles to move a body covered with such heavy armor. Today we would probably be harnessing that power. *Ankylosaurus* would make an ideal beast of burden, rather like the elephants of India today.

Ankylosaurus

Classification Thyreophorans—the armored dinosaurs. They were divided into two lines—the stegosaurs with sticking-up plates and spikes, and the ankylosaurs with armor across their backs.

Fossil finds Texas, Wyoming USA; Alberta, Canada.

Habitat Forest.

Name *Ankylosaurus*, meaning "fused lizard."

Physical characteristics A heavily-built armored dinosaur with a bony club on the end of its tail.

Time Late Cretaceous period, 70 – 65 million years ago.

KILLER TAIL

Ankylosaurus was the biggest of the armored dinosaurs. Its head was a solid box of armored bone. Its back was covered in armor plates right down to the end of its tail where there was a club made from heavy chunks of bone. The tail was stiff and straight, like the shaft of a medieval mace. The club at the end could be swung with force against the legs of an attacker.

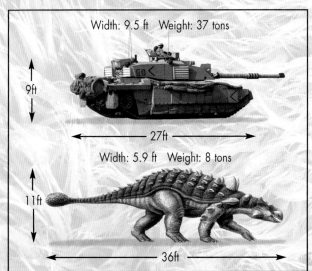

TANK vs ADULT *ANKYLOSAURUS*

Width: 9.5 ft   Weight: 37 tons

9ft

27ft

Width: 5.9 ft   Weight: 8 tons

11ft

36ft

Ankylosaurus had thick armor that was almost impossible for a predator to bite through. In a similar way, a tank's armor protects it from gun and missile fire.

The Longest Dinosaur

Chaos at the airport! A herd of *Seismosaurus* has wandered on to a runway. All traffic is brought to a halt as the great beasts wander unconcerned amongst the aircraft. It will take the security and maintenance services some time to move these obstructions.

Open areas, such as airport runways, would be a familiar habitat to the big sauropods like *Seismosaurus*. They lived on the arid open landscapes of Late Jurassic North America, feeding on the trees that grew along the sides of rivers. They would not be disturbed by the movement of taxiing aircraft, as to them they would be just like other big sauropods to which they are accustomed.

Seismosaurus

Classification Diplodocid sauropods—the long and slender group of long-necked plant-eaters that were the main herbivores of the Late Jurassic period.

Fossil finds Montana, USA; Alberta, Canada.

Habitat Riverside forest.

Name *Seismosaurus*, meaning "earthquake lizard."

Physical characteristics Sauropod with an elephantine body and a very long neck and tail.

Time Late Jurassic period, 83 – 70 million years ago.

A SIZEABLE FIND

When the single-known skeleton of *Seismosaurus* was found, it was celebrated as the longest dinosaur that ever existed, with an estimated length of about 150 feet. But the skeleton was incomplete. Today we do not think that it was quite so long. Some scientists think that it was just a large species of its close relative, *Diplodocus*.

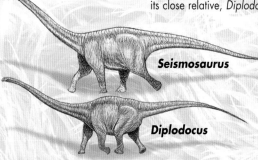

Seismosaurus

Diplodocus

SAUROPOD vs HUMAN

6ft
5ft
4ft
3ft
2ft
1ft
0ft

All of *Seismosaurus'* bones were long! Although this leg bone (femur) is from a *Diplodocus*, *Seismosaurus'* would have been a similarly huge size.

Herd Mentality

A patter of three-toed feet on the turf. A flock of *Psittacosaurus* bunch together as predators circle. In a herd, they take protection from one another. One of their group miscalculates and splits away from the flock. In its Cretaceous home this would make it vulnerable, but here the "menace" is from trained sheepdogs, and soon it is guided back to its companions.

It may well be that small plant-eating dinosaurs such as *Psittacosaurus* would be easy to breed, and so become important farm animals in the modern world. However, the herding instinct would still exist in them—it is a valuable survival mechanism. Threatened by meat-eating dinosaurs, small plant-eaters like *Psittacosaurus* would find safety in a group.
  With lots of animals crowded together, perhaps only one would be killed by the attackers, and the rest would be safe.

Psittacosaurus

Fossil finds Mongolia, China, and Thailand.

Name *Psittacosaurus* meaning "parrot lizard."

Time Early Cretaceous period, about 120 — 95 million years ago.

Classification
Marginocephalians—dinosaurs with head ornaments. Within this group the psittacosaurids were small, two-footed types, with heavy beaks giving them parrot-like heads.

Habitat Desert and scrubland.

Physical characteristics
Long legs and short arms, it walked on two legs. A square-shaped skull with a parrot-like beak. About 6.5 feet long.

PARENT AND CHILD GROUP

This picture shows a group of *Psittacosaurus* young that were found with a parent in Liaoning, China, in 2004. It was a significant discovery because not many fossils of dinosaurs looking after their young have been found.

PARROT HEAD

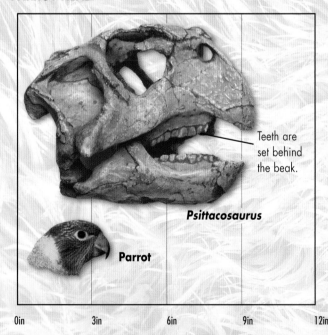

Teeth are set behind the beak.

Psittacosaurus

Parrot

| 0in | 3in | 6in | 9in | 12in |

Psittacosaurus' head and beak were similarly shaped to a parrot's. However, unlike a parrot, the *Psittacosaurus* also had teeth to eat with.

Lives of the Plant-Eaters

How could such enormous and complex creatures survive in today's world? It would be difficult…

They would probably be blundering around, causing substantial chaos. There may not even be enough food to sustain these massive animals. It is likely that we would have found practical uses for them…

Seismosaurus

There are always more plant-eating animals than meat-eaters. On the African savannah today you would see whole herds of Seismosaurus, but only a handful of lions or cheetahs.

Araucaria tree

As with all animals, the plant-eating dinosaurs developed along with the food that they ate. Short-needled conifers, such as the redwoods and cypresses that we see today, adapted with prosauropods (ancestors of sauropods like *Seismosaurus*). So, herbivores could happily exist where these trees grow today. However, these conifers are not as abundant as they were in dinosaur times. They are mostly found in high altitudes, and mountains. These areas are probably the ones in which long-necked plant-eaters would thrive today,

if they could stand the cold. If they couldn't, our only chance to see them would probably be in captivity.

But would it be practical to keep such big animals in a zoo or safari park? In the real world, we love to see big animals up close. If we were to keep herbivores in captivity, their specialist diet would be very important. Whole groves of *Araucaria* trees or redwoods would have to be planted and grown to maturity before a captive sauropod family could be established. And this would take decades. Entertainment value aside,

these plant-eaters would be farmed as our main source of food. Traditional livestock such as cows, sheep and pigs would be classed as wild animals and rarely seen, like deer today.

We have found the remains of grasses in a specimen of sauropod dung, so we know that they did eat grass at some time. But grass never became a major part of the dinosaur diet. There was very little grass at the time of the dinosaurs, wide grasslands did not develop until after the dinosaurs had died out. Today, who knows? Perhaps dinosaurs would adapt to eat this abundant plant. In which case they would be as plentiful today as they were millions of years ago.

Triceratops

However, grass is very tough stuff to eat. That is why modern grass-eating animals, like horses and antelope, have strong teeth and very complex digestive systems. If dinosaurs adapted to eat grass, they would have to develop these strong teeth

and complex innards as well. In fact they would probably not look very much like the familiar dinosaurs at all.

The other main group of plant-eating dinosaurs were the ornithischian group. These consisted of two-footed ornithopods, plated stegosaurs, armored ankylosaurs and horned ceratopsians. They had a beak at the front of the mouth, used for gathering food, and specialized teeth at the back for crushing or chopping. They could eat a bigger variety of plants, and so today the ornithischians would be much more successful than the sauropods. The larger of these animals would be well-used as sturdy beasts of burden today.

The dinosaurs that we know and love would be very restricted in their distribution, especially as humans have spread into just about every habitat on the globe. It would be difficult for dinosaurs and humans to cohabit happily.

Modern Grasses
Grass is very tough stuff to eat. The leaves are almost indigestible and are full of grains of silica, so it is like chewing sandpaper.

A Terrible Tyrant

Wild cattle are grazing peacefully on the open plains. Suddenly one animal senses danger and snorts a warning. The herd scatters. A mighty *Tyrannosaurus* has been lying in wait for them. It is now bearing down on them, its three foot-long jaws, armed with six inch teeth, opening for the kill. A film crew captures the scene from a helicopter above.

Many palaeontologists believe that this is how the fearsome predator *Tyrannosaurus* hunted its prey. Others think *Tyrannosaurus* was too big and heavy to chase its prey, and would have feasted on the corpses of animals that had already died. The most likely story is that both of these theories are true — *Tyrannosaurus* was an active hunter, but would not have missed the chance to scavenge on carrion, or steal a meal from a rival predator. Whatever its choice of food, *Tyrannosaurus* would probably find itself hunted to extinction by farmers trying to protect their livestock.

Tyrannosaurus

Fossil finds Montana, South Dakota, Wyoming and Texas, USA; Alberta, Canada. About 20 *Tyrannosaurus* specimens have been found in total.

Name *Tyrannosaurus*, meaning "tyrant reptile."

Time Late Cretaceous period, 74 – 65 million years ago.

Classification Tyrannosaurids — amongst the last of the meat-eating theropods. The earliest members of this family (alive during the Jurassic period) were turkey-sized animals. But by the Late Cretaceous period, the tyrannosaurid family had evolved to include some of the biggest meat-eaters ever known.

Habitat Forest or flood plains.

Physical characteristics Short, deep and solid skull with eyes positioned for stereoscopic view.

TYRANNOSAURUS SKULL

The skull of *Tyrannosaurus* was massive with a mouth that could hold a whole wildebeest. *Tyrannosaurus'* powerful jaws and teeth could penetrate the thick skin of a dinosaur, such as *Triceratops*, and crunch through its bones in a single bite.

TYRANT TEETH

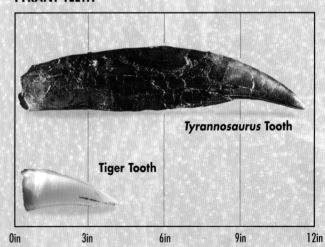

Tyrannosaurus Tooth

Tiger Tooth

0in   3in   6in   9in   12in

A *Tyrannosaurus* cheek tooth could grow up to 11 inches long, including the root—up to four times the length of a modern predator's.

Scary Scavengers

In the darkness of a dank smelly night, scavenging beasts sniff around the waste of a city. Foxes, once rural hunters, have become urban scavengers, finding food wherever it is discarded by people. But they are not alone—small dinosaurs such as *Coelophysis*, once rural hunters themselves, have also turned to scavenging ways. These young *Coelophysis* are prepared to challenge the larger fox for the prize of a stolen meal.

Although *Coelophysis* had the build of a fast and agile hunter, it would have been perfectly happy to eat any dead food that happened to be lying around. Today it would be an urban scavenger and would therefore be in competition with the foxes and rats of our cities.

Coelophysis

Fossil finds Arizona and New Mexico, USA.

Name *Coelophysis*, meaning "hollow form."

Time Late Triassic period, 228 – 200 million years ago.

Classification Coelophysids— an early and primitive group of the meat-eating theropods. They were lightly-built with slim legs and had an active lifestyle. They lived worldwide in the early part of the Age of Dinosaurs.

Habitat Arid landscapes and oases.

Physical characteristics Small, lightweight meat-eater with longish jaws, a long neck and long tail.

COMPETING HUNTERS AND SCAVENGERS

Coelophysis was not the only efficient meat-eating dinosaur around at the beginning of the Age of Dinosaurs. Most of the other meat-eaters were active lightweight animals as well. They would all have been competing for the same food, whether they were hunting for small living things like lizards or crocodiles, or scavenging from the corpses of dead animals.

SKILLFUL HUNTERS

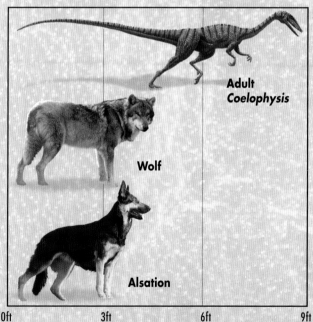

Adult *Coelophysis*

Wolf

Alsation

| 0ft | 3ft | 6ft | 9ft |

Coelophysis hunted in packs like modern wolves and dogs. It would not have eaten as much, though, as mammals need more food to support their warm-blooded lifestyle.

Heavy Claw

A rush of water through the rapids and over the falls. The silvery leap of a salmon as it migrates. A snap! And it is caught in mid-air by an alert grizzly bear. Then another snap! And a *Baryonyx* has closed its jaws on the same fish. It is an unequal struggle, and the stronger dinosaur takes its prize away from the disappointed mammal.

When its skeleton was found, *Baryonyx* immediately attracted a huge amount of interest. Nothing like it was known. It had a big claw on its hand, and long narrow jaws with small crocodile-like teeth. When the fossils of fish remains were found in its stomach, scientists realized that it must have hunted fish like a grizzly bear, hooking them out with its big claw or snapping them up in its big mouth. *Baryonyx* would take its place alongside bears and herons, amongst the hunters of fish in modern streams and rivers.

Baryonyx

Fossil finds Southern England.

Name *Baryonyx*, meaning "heavy claw."

Time Early Cretaceous period, 130 – 125 million years ago.

Classification Spinosaurids— the group of meat-eating theropods with long jaws and sails on their backs. Some scientists now think that *Baryonyx* may have had a sail.

Habitat River banks.

Physical characteristics Long, very narrow jaws, with lots of small sharp teeth. An enormous claw on its thumb.

BIG CLAW

The first part of a *Baryonyx* skeleton to be found was its huge claw. This was on the first finger of its hand. It would have been used to hook fish out of shallow water, as grizzly bears do today. The rest of the skeleton was eventually found. In its stomach were fish scales and fish bones, showing that fish were its main food. There were also dinosaur bones in there, proving that *Baryonyx* ate bigger prey too.

FISH HUNTERS

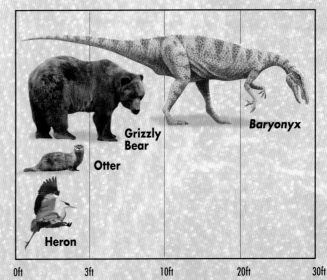

Grizzly Bear

Otter

Heron

Baryonyx

| 0ft | 3ft | 10ft | 20ft | 30ft |

None of the freshwater fish-hunting animals from our modern world—not even the largest grizzly bear—can begin to compare in size to *Baryonyx*.

Pack Hunters

Bounding across the outback comes a red kangaroo—its strong hind legs and balancing tail making it the fastest plant-eater around. However, it is no match for the equally fast *Troodon* pair that converge, hounding it with their sharply-clawed hands, their killer-clawed toes and their steak knife-like teeth.

By the Cretaceous period there were many fast-running plant-eaters. As a result, fleet-footed predators evolved. *Troodon*, with its long, slim cheetah-like legs was one of them. Their natural prey would have been the sprinting hypsilophodonts—fast plant-eaters that were about *Troodon's* size. In today's world where there are fleet-footed plant-eaters like kangaroos, there will always be room for fleet-footed carnivores, like *Troodon*.

Troodon

Fossil finds Montana and Wyoming, USA; Alberta, Canada.

Name *Troodon*, meaning "wounding tooth."

Time Late Cretaceous period, 80 – 65 million years ago.

Classification Troodontids— one of the later and most bird-like of the theropods. They were members of the coelurosaurid group—those with lightweight bones and a stiff tail to balance them while running.

Habitat Open plains.

Physical characteristics Slim body, long legs and three fingered hands. Large brain for its body size.

NESTS AND EGGS

Troodon is a close relative of birds. It made nests to protect its eggs. The nests were quite simple, just an oval ridge of mud. The eggs were laid in pairs. This suggests that female *Troodons* had a pair of egg tubes in their bodies; whereas modern birds have just one egg tube. Birds have developed many features which keep their weight down and make flying easier. While *Troodon* was covered with downy, short feathers, they were used to keep the animal warm, they were not for flying.

BIG BRAIN

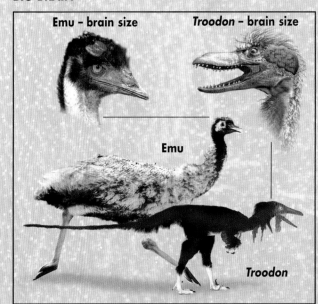

Emu – brain size Troodon – brain size

Emu

Troodon

Troodon had the largest brain in relation to its body of all the dinosaurs. Although its body size is comparable to the modern emu, its brain was far larger.

The World's Fastest Dinosaur

The crowds are cheering as the jockeys push the racehorses on and on. However, years of fitness training are not enough to match the natural speed of the flock of *Struthiomimus* that have joined the race. These slender, long-legged dinosaurs are effortlessly reaching speeds of 50 miles an hour—an essential survival skill for animals that lived alongside giant carnivores such as *Tyrannosaurus* and *Giganotosaurus*.

The speed of *Struthiomimus* at a sprint may well have led to its inclusion in modern sporting fixtures. *Struthiomimus* resembled today's large flightless birds, such as ostriches and emus, and were the ancestors of all modern-day birds. They lived and hunted in packs and had large brains in relation to their body size suggesting they were not only fast runners, but clever too!

Struthiomimus

Fossil finds United States of America; Alberta, Canada.

Name *Struthiomimus* meaning "ostrich mimic."

Time Late Cretaceous period, 97 – 65 million years ago.

Classification
Ornithomimid—the "bird mimics," a group of theropods. They had plump, compact bodies; big eyes which would have spotted danger coming from far away, and long running legs.

Habitat Open plains.

Physical characteristics
Small two-footed dinosaur with a toothless jaw, and a long neck.

LONG TAIL

The dinosaur's long tail can clearly be seen in this image of a fossilized *Struthiomimus*. The long tail balanced the dinosaur as it ran at high speeds, and gave it the maneuverability to swerve and turn quickly to avoid danger.

BUILT FOR SPEED

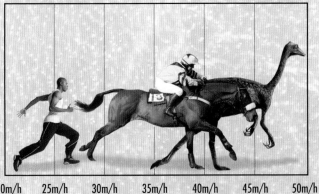

| 0m/h | 25m/h | 30m/h | 35m/h | 40m/h | 45m/h | 50m/h |

Struthiomimus may have been the world's fastest dinosaur. It could outrun many of today's animals.

The Silent Thief

A quiet November morning on Christmas Island is interrupted by shrill cries from a flock of *Oviraptor*. The island's juvenile red crabs have left the safety of their forest home and begun their annual migration to the sea. For these feathered dinosaurs, Christmas has come early and they excitedly communicate news of the feast to each other.

Birds are closely related to *Oviraptor*. However its diet was more varied because of its strong beak and powerful jaws. It could easily crunch through shell and bone. Shellfish like these crabs would be easy prey for the *Oviraptor*.

TEMPORARY REQUEST
DUE TO MIGRATING CRABS

Australian
Nature
Conservation
Agency

SHIRE OF CHRISTMAS ISLAND

WOULD ALL MOTORISTS
PLEASE FOLLOW THE
RECOMMENDATION BELOW

AVOID USING THIS ROAD IF POSSIBLE

Oviraptor

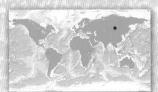

Fossil finds Mongolia, Asia.

Name *Oviraptor*, meaning "egg thief."

Time Late Cretaceous period, 83 – 70 million years ago.

Classification Oviraptorid—a group of theropods with thick, bird-like beaks that were probably covered in feathers.

Habitat Deserts.

Physical characteristics A turkey-sized theropod, with a short face and a heavy toothless beak, and a crest on top if its head. Its skeleton was very bird-like, so some scientists think it should be regarded as a kind of bird.

EGG-STEALER

Oviraptor was always thought to have been an egg-stealer, slinking around other dinosaur's nests and stealing their eggs and young. This was because the first *Oviraptor* skeleton found was close to a nesting site that was thought to have belonged to the horned dinosaur, *Protoceratops*. Then, fifty years later, an *Oviraptor* skeleton was found actually sitting on a nest of these eggs. It had died in a sandstorm while incubating them. They were the nests of *Oviraptor* all along.

IS IT A BIRD...?

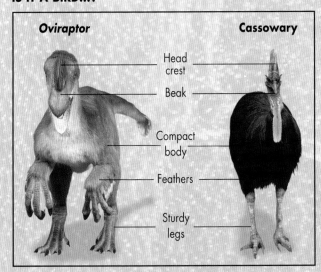

Oviraptor

Cassowary

Head crest

Beak

Compact body

Feathers

Sturdy legs

Several physical features of *Oviraptor* have led scientists to believe that it is closely related to modern birds, such as the Cassowary.

A Fallen Giant

A *Ceratosaurus* desperately tries to defend itself but the big hunter is not always invulnerable. Even something as fierce as *Ceratosaurus* could find itself the victim of more powerful or better-organized predators. An elderly or sickly *Ceratosaurus* would be easy prey to a pride of hungry lions.

On the Jurassic plains, *Ceratosaurus* was a successful medium-sized hunter—a force to contend with amongst the long-necked sauropods and the two-footed ornithopods of the time. However, there were also other hunters around, such as *Allosaurus* which was bigger and stronger than *Ceratosaurus*; and *Ornitholestes* which was smaller and probably hunted in packs. They would probably all have been in competition for the same food. Like the tiger, *Ceratosaurus* would probably be a protected animal, despite being distrusted by people who live in its hunting area.

Ceratosaurus

Fossil finds Colorado and Utah, USA; with a potential specimen from Tanzania, Africa.

Name *Ceratosaurus*, meaning "horned lizard."

Time Late Jurassic period, 155 – 150 million years ago.

Classification Neoceratosauria —the group of meat-eating theropod dinosaurs characterized by very flexible tails. Despite being quite primitive they gave rise to groups that lasted until the end of the Age of Dinosaurs.

Habitat Riverside woodlands.

Physical characteristics Medium-sized, meat-eating dinosaur with a horn on its snout, another pair above the eyes, and a jagged crest down its back.

BIG TEETH

The skull of *Ceratosaurus* is a lightweight structure made up of thin struts of bone surrounding huge holes—just like the skulls of most dinosaurs. The feature that makes it different, apart from the horns, is the enormous size of its teeth—they are far bigger in proportion to the size of the skull than those of other theropods.

CERATOSAURUS' DINNER

Antelope

Crocodile

Trout

Ceratosaurus may have had the most varied diet of any dinosaur. It is thought to have hunted and scavenged a wide variety of animals.

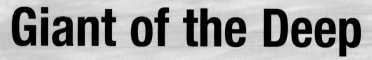

Giant of the Deep

From the dark depths of the ocean a mighty *Shonisaurus* rises towards the pale blue glow of the upper waters. Its watchful eye spots a giant octopus, lazily flapping along, with a bunching and opening of its tentacles. The great jaws close, and the giant octopus is gone.

The ichthyosaurs were the fish-shaped reptiles of the Age of Dinosaurs. The earliest ones seem to have been the largest. In the Triassic period they were as enormous as sperm whales. They probably lived like sperm whales as well, eating the biggest of the marine invertebrates of the time. A huge one, like *Shonisaurus*, would find plenty to eat in today's oceans.

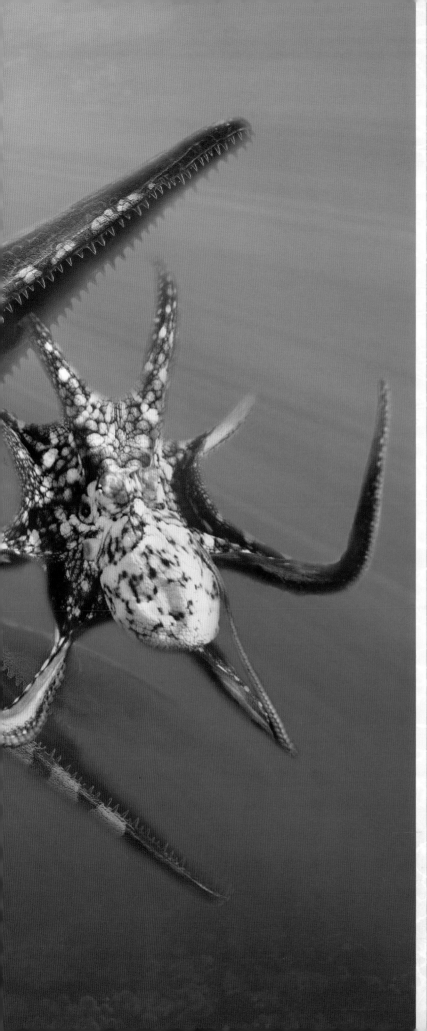

Shonisaurus

Fossil finds Nevada, USA; British Columbia, Canada.

Name *Shonisaurus*, meaning "lizard from the Shoshone mountains."

Time Late Triassic period, 216 – 213 million years ago.

Classification Ichthyosaurids— the "fish-lizards." They were highly adapted to life at sea— with fish-shaped bodies, paddles and fins instead of legs, and an ability to give birth in water.

Habitat Open oceans.

Physical characteristics Very large ichthyosaur with big eyes and rigid paddles.

SEA MONSTER

A *Shonisaurus* skeleton found in 1998 in British Columbia was so big that it could only be seen in its entirety from the air. There were other monster ichthyosaurs in the Triassic seas. Obviously something about the oceans in Triassic times encouraged the growth of these very big creatures. The ichthyosaurs existed for another 120 million years, after this period. But the later ichthyosaurs were more modest dolphin-sized animals.

MODERN GIANTS

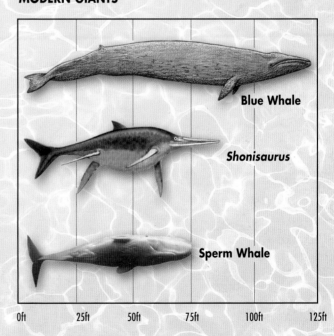

People think that prehistoric animals were bigger than anything alive today. As you can see from this chart, that's not true. The blue whale is still the biggest ocean creature ever to have existed.

Earth's Largest Killer

As seals bask close to the shore an orca suddenly beaches to attack the unsuspecting animals. Unsuccessful, the orca prepares to slide back into the water with the pull of the next wave, but slowly and silently an even bigger predator moves close. Suddenly the water seems to boil as the vast jaws of *Liopleurodon* break the surface and the largest hunter the world has ever known moves in for the kill.

Dwarfing even the sperm whale, the biggest predator in the ocean today, *Liopleurodon* cruised the Jurassic seas propelled by four large flippers. This giant pliosaur was a powerful swimmer and its massive jaws and huge teeth made it a fearsome hunter. *Liopleurodon* had only one enemy—its own kind! Like today's sperm whales, orcas and great white sharks, it was the top predator in its habitat, killing and eating any other living thing that came within its reach. It would probably be the top predator in today's oceans.

Liopleurodon

Classification Pliosauroids— a group of sea-living reptiles, with huge heads and short necks. They were related to the long-necked plesiosauroids, but totally unrelated to dinosaurs.

Fossil finds United Kingdom; France; Germany; Eastern Europe; Chile, South America.

Habitat The shallow seas that covered most of Northern Europe.

Name *Liopleurodon* meaning "smooth-sided tooth."

Physical Characteristics Broad bodies, short tails and two pairs of wing-like paddles.

Time Late Jurassic period, 160 – 155 million years ago.

THE SCENT OF A KILL

Liopleurodon could smell prey in the water. Palaeontologists believe it swam with its mouth open, allowing water to pass up into scoop-shaped openings in the roof of its mouth. The water was then passed out through small nostrils in front of its eyes. Like a modern great white shark, which can smell one drop of blood in 25 gallons of water, *Liopleurodon* could probably smell a potential meal from a great distance.

PREDATOR OR PREY?

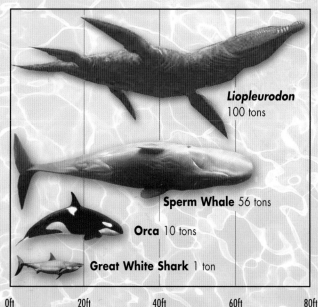

Liopleurodon 100 tons

Sperm Whale 56 tons

Orca 10 tons

Great White Shark 1 ton

| 0ft | 20ft | 40ft | 60ft | 80ft |

Scientists cannot yet agree on how big *Liopleurodon* might have grown, but many believe it reached 78 feet long. If *Liopleurodon* were alive today, the ocean's largest predators, such as orcas, would become its prey!

Prehistoric Seashells

A sea otter surfaces in its rocky inlet. After a brief underwater hunt it brings up an ammonite—a tentacled mollusk in a coiled shell. Used to dealing with hard-shelled animals like oysters and scallops, the otter will find little difficulty in breaking into the shell and extracting the flesh.

Imagine an octopus in a coiled shell, that is what an ammonite looked like. Ammonites were amongst the commonest sea creatures during the Age of Dinosaurs. There were a vast range of shapes and sizes, with different lifestyles ranging from fast hunters to drifting filter feeders. In modern oceans they would probably be as plentiful as they were back then.

Ammonite

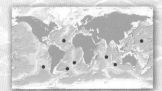

Classification Cephalopoda—a family of mollusks that have tentacles like octopuses and squid; from the mollusk group of shelled invertebrates.

Fossil finds Worldwide.

Name Ammonite, from the Egyptian god Ammon who had a pair of curled goat's horns.

Time From Triassic to the Cretaceous periods, 250 – 65 million years ago.

Habitat Open ocean.

Physical characteristics Octopus-like animal in a coiled shell. Thousands of different species with various patterned shells.

FLOATING SHELLFISH

Ammonites are extinct today, but during the Age of the Dinosaurs the seas were full of them. They mostly drifted in the water, adjusting their

buoyancy by filling chambers in their shells with air. This picture shows the cross-section of an ammonite with its chambers exposed.

SPECIES AGE CHART

Quartenary Period Present Day	**Nautilus**
Cretaceous Period 135 – 65 MYA	**Ammonite**
Jurassic Period 135 – 65 MYA	**Ammonite**
Triassic Period 250 – 203 MYA	**Ammonite**

*MYA = Million Years Ago

The nautilus is a relative of prehistoric ammonites. It successfully existed during the same periods, relatively unchanged, while ammonites became extinct.

Caught Up

A drift net closes around a shoal of ammonites. The swimming mollusks bunch together as the walls of their trap close around them. Then the net is gathered and the whole catch is lifted from the water. But ammonites are not the only things caught. A *Mosasaurus*—a swimming lizard that had been hunting the ammonites—is tangled in the net as well. An unwitting victim of the fishing industry.

The mosasaurs were closely related to today's monitor lizards, but were totally aquatic. We know that they ate ammonites because we have found fossil ammonite shells that had been bitten many times and crushed by mosasaur jaws, while the reptile extracted the soft-bodied animal from within. They would be as at home in modern oceans as they were at the end of the Age of Dinosaurs.

Mosasaurus

Fossil finds Netherlands, but closely related animals are found worldwide.

Name *Mosasaurus*, meaning "lizard from the Meuse"—the Netherlands river where the first specimen was found.

Time Late Cretaceous period, 70 – 65 million years ago.

Classification Mosasaurids— a group of extinct sea reptiles very closely related to modern monitor lizards. They were the most powerful hunters at the end of the Age of Dinosaurs, taking the place of the ichthyosaurids after they died out.

Habitat Open ocean.

Physical characteristics Like a giant monitor lizard, but with a flattened swimming tail and paddles instead of feet.

THE FIRST BIG REPTILE FOSSIL

Before dinosaurs were discovered, people found the remains of some very big, extinct sea animals. This picture shows one of the most famous. It was dug up in a Dutch quarry in 1780 and named *Mosasaurus*. It became seized in a subsequent war and was taken to Paris as booty. It was studied there by the most famous naturalist of the day, Baron Georges Cuvier.

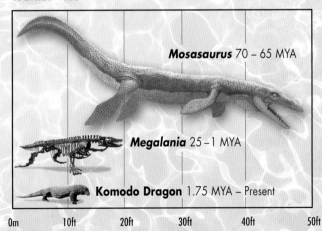

FAMILY TIES

Mosasaurus 70 – 65 MYA

Megalania 25 –1 MYA

Komodo Dragon 1.75 MYA – Present

0m	10ft	20ft	30ft	40ft	50ft

The prehistoric *Mosasaurus* is a relative of the Ice Age *Megalania*, and the Komodo dragon that is found in Indonesia today. Whereas the *Mosasaurus* was a sea-dwelling animal, the others are land animals.

Chilling Out

Tourists watch the sea lions on the decks of a marina. They even encourage them by throwing scraps of fish. But now the plesiosaur *Cryptoclidus* has learned of this, and it is coming to the marina too, for an easy meal.

Cryptoclidus was one of the long-necked plesiosaurs. These lived and hunted rather like modern sea lions, "flying" through the water with their wing-like paddles, and snapping up fish with their long sharp teeth. Also like sea lions, they probably came ashore to breed. It would not be surprising if they also became used to human presence and adopted habits that we usually associate with marine mammals.

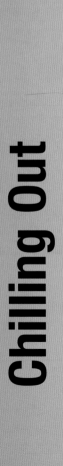

Cryptoclidus

Fossil finds England; France; Russia; South America.

Name *Cryptoclidus* meaning "hidden collar-bone."

Time Middle Jurassic period, 160 – 165 million years ago.

Classification Plesiosauroids— the swimming reptiles, related to the pliosauroids but with long-necks and small heads. They existed throughout the Age of Dinosaurs. They shared the oceans with the ichthyosaurids and then the mosasaurids.

Habitat Shallow seas.

Physical characteristics A solid body about 13 feet long. Its neck was not very flexible. It used four broad paddles to push itself through the water. Long, sharp, needle-like teeth for catching fish.

MASTER OF DISGUISE

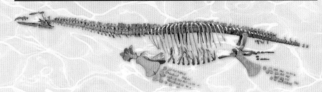

Scientists believe that *Cryptoclidus'* small head and long neck helped it to sneak up on prey. Potential prey were not threatened by its small head. Its long neck kept its large body out of sight—until it was too late for them to realize they were dinner! *Cryptoclidus* seems to have mostly eaten squid and fish.

FILTER FEEDING

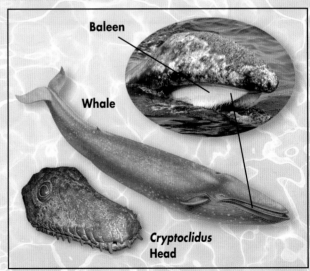

Baleen

Whale

Cryptoclidus Head

Cryptoclidus had many interlocking needle-like teeth that may have been used to filter its food from water—in the same way some whales use plates of bone, called baleen, in their mouths.

Lives of the Ocean-Dwellers

"Danger!
Bathing beach closed.
Pliosaurs sighted!"

Would our beaches be inundated with warning signs like this? Or would these creatures have been hunted to the brink of extinction?

Ammonite
These shellfish could be harvested as a human food resource.

The physical danger that we would face from giant sea reptiles, if they existed today, would be real, but probably quite rare. After all, how many reports of shark attacks do we read about nowadays?

Green Turtle

The first land-living animals descended directly from sea-living creatures. However, it was not long before this development was reversed. Some land animals re-adapted to become sea-living animals once more. Plesiosaurs were one such animal. Like turtles, plesiosaurs would have to come ashore to lay eggs.

Today, beaches in some areas would be designated as plesiosaur nesting beaches and protected. However, there would always be poachers, willing to risk danger and imprisonment to gain either the nourishment, or funds, offered by a clutch of plesiosaur eggs.

Amongst the reptiles, the ichthyosaurs may have adapted best to modern sea-life.

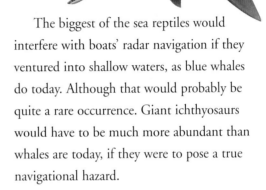

Ichthyosaur
Medium-sized swimming reptiles such as these would be great for sport fishing! Their cunning and strength would easily match a human's skill.

If you saw an ichthyosaur in the distance you would think it was a dolphin, or a shark. It had the same streamlined shape, half-moon fin on the tail and triangular fin on the back. It also gave birth to live young in the water. These factors alone suggest its survival in today's world would be guaranteed.

We can also imagine the danger to shipping caused by big reptiles swimming close to the surface. A large-bodied plesiosaur just below the surface could be a problem for pleasure boats or small fishing boats. The current thinking about the plesiosaur is that it swam just beneath the waves, and reached downwards with its neck to catch fish swimming below it. If this was so, motor-powered boats would be more of a threat to the plesiosaurs than vice versa. Manatees in shallow Caribbean waters are often injured or killed, by speed boat propellers. It is very likely that plesiosaurs would suffer the same fate.

Manatee

The biggest of the sea reptiles would interfere with boats' radar navigation if they ventured into shallow waters, as blue whales do today. Although that would probably be quite a rare occurrence. Giant ichthyosaurs would have to be much more abundant than whales are today, if they were to pose a true navigational hazard.

But what about the smaller ocean animals from the Age of Dinosaurs? If they were present in the same numbers as in the Mesozoic Era, then they would make up a significant part of the ecosystem. If they were found to be edible to humans, then a whole specialist fishing industry would have been built around their capture and processing. Ammonite sushi, anyone? Ammonite and chips?

If all these exotic animals existed today, they would be faced with the same problems that face modern animals. They may be over-fished or over-hunted. Who knows, there may even be a "Save the ichthyosaur!" campaign.

SAVE THE ICHTHYOSAUR!

The Early Bird

A bald eagle, king of the skies, is flying back to its nest with a lizard. Suddenly it is set upon by a trio of arrogant *Archaeopteryx*. The eagle clutches its prize.

As the earliest-known bird, *Archaeopteryx* shows features of both modern birds and its ancestors, reptiles—it appears to attack its descendant so that it can eat its ancestor! *Archaeopteryx* would look very odd today. Its body, jaws and tail were those of a small dinosaur, but it was covered in feathers and had wings that were almost identical in structure to those of modern birds. There is no doubt at all that this mixture of features show that birds were descended from reptiles, in particular dinosaurs. Whether or not *Archaeopteryx* would survive in the modern environment, alongside its more highly adapted descendants, is not at all clear.

Archaeopteryx

Classification Bird—the most primitive known. It was almost like a dinosaur, but it had feathers and well-formed flying wings. It is proof that modern birds descended from dinosaurs.

Fossil finds Solnhofen, Germany.

Habitat Arid islands.

Name *Archaeopteryx*, meaning "ancient wing."

Physical characteristics The size of a pigeon, with the wings and feathers of a bird, but the jaw, hands and tail of a dinosaur.

Time Late Jurassic period, 155 — 15 million years ago.

A HALFWAY STAGE

If we found the fossil of *Archaeopteryx* without the feathers we would think it was a little dinosaur. In fact one of the only eight specimens found was misidentified as a dinosaur for years. It is hard evidence that birds descended from dinosaurs.

Wings

WING FORM

Looking closely at these two wings, it is difficult to tell which belongs to a prehistoric *Archaeopteryx* and which to a modern hawk. The layout of the feathers is the same, as are the shapes of the feathers themselves. The only major difference is the fact that the *Archaeopteryx* wing has fingers.

Fingers

Archaeopteryx

Modern Hawk

The Super Vulture

For several miles now the pilot of a small passenger plane has been trying to outmaneuver a huge pair of *Quetzalcoatlus*. He may have flown too close to their nest, or they may just be enjoying the thrill of a chase. As the pilot banks to avoid making contact with them he notices another plane ahead. The situation is getting quite dangerous...

Amongst the pterosaurs, *Quetzalcoatlus* was one of the biggest, with a wingspan exceeding that of a hang glider and even some powered aircraft. Most pterosaur fossils have been found by the sea, leaving us to believe that this was their primary habitat. *Quetzalcoatlus*, however, lived well inland, where it was able to use rising air thermals from the warm, open landscape to keep it aloft for vast distances. *Quetzalcoatlus* would dominate the skies today, and probably compete with vultures for dead animals on the ground.

Quetzalcoatlus

Fossil finds Texas, USA

Name *Quetzalcoatlus*: from Quetzalcoatl, a flying serpent-god in Aztec mythology.

Time Late Cretaceous period, 70 — 65 million years ago.

Classification
Pterodactyloidea—the more advanced group of pterosaurs with short tails. Pterosaurs were the flying reptiles of the Age of Dinosaurs.

Habitat The sky, over open plains.

Physical characteristics
A very large pterosaur, with a wingspan of up to 36 feet.

GLIDER

The exact wingspan of *Quetzalcoatlus* is unknown. Only part of a wing skeleton has been found, which suggests a wingspan of between 39 and 59 feet. Despite being such a huge animal, the *Quetzalcoatlus* is thought to have weighed only around 220 pounds.

WINGING IT

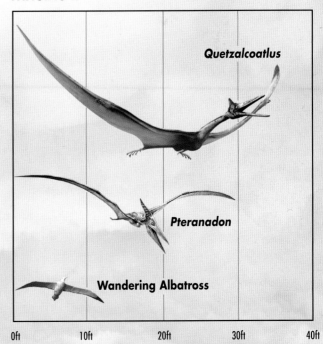

Quetzalcoatlus

Pteranadon

Wandering Albatross

| 0ft | 10ft | 20ft | 30ft | 40ft |

The albatross has the biggest wingspan of any modern bird— 12 feet. However, even it would be dwarfed by the size of the biggest pterosaurs.

Territorial Threat

At a bird-feeder, a little bird's meal of seeds is rudely interrupted. A pair of *Anurognathus* swoop down and chase it away. Although *Anurognathus* is an insect-feeder not a seed-eater, it is very protective of its territory.

When the dinosaurs were alive, the air was full of pterosaurs—the flying reptiles. If they were around today they would have to compete with the birds for their food. Like the modern birds, there were many shapes and sizes of pterosaur, each type having a different lifestyle and eating a different food. *Anurognathus* was the pterosaur equivalent of the swift—a fast aerial hunter of insects.

Anurognathus

Classification
Rhamphorhynchoids—the most primitive of the pterosaurs. Pterosaurs were the flying reptiles of the Age of Dinosaurs.

Fossil finds Germany.

Name *Anurognathus* meaning "jaws but no tail."

Time Late Jurassic period, 150 – 145 million years ago.

Habitat In the air over shallow tropical lagoons.

Physical characteristics
The smallest pterosaur known, and although it was a rhamphorhynchoid, usually long-tailed, it had a tail that was just a stump.

AN AGILE FLIER

Although there was only one specimen of *Anurognathus* found, back in 1923, we know of its wing membrane because so many of its relatives such as *Pterodactylus* have been found in the very fine-grained lithographic limestone of southern Germany. The preservation was so good that the imprint of the skin of the wings was preserved. In fine lake deposits in Kazakhstan we find fossils of related pterosaurs in which even the fur of the body is preserved.

BILL ADAPTATIONS

Crossbill

Hornbill

Stork

Anurognathus

Different pterosaurs had differently-shaped jaws depending on their diet and lifestyle—just as different types of birds today have differently-shaped beaks.

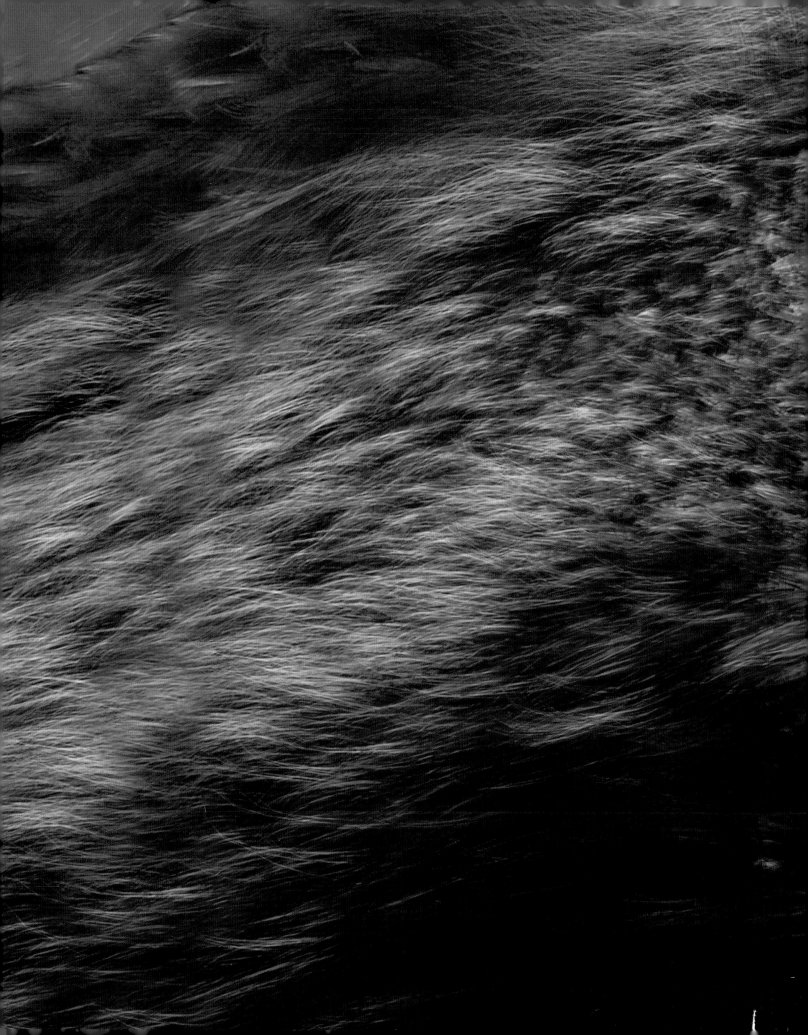

Clinging On

Spots? On the face of the Statue of Liberty? No, not spots, but a flock of the tiny flying dinosaur—*Microraptor*. With wing feathers on both the arms and the legs, *Microraptor* is a very efficient glider. Its four wings use the rising air thermals to lift it to considerable heights and its long claws allow it to cling to the faces of tall buildings.

In Early Cretaceous times *Microraptor* was just one of several half-bird, half-dinosaur animals. If we saw a flock of *Microraptor* swirling in the slanting sunlight, we would think that they were birds, or even big butterflies. We do not know what color their plumage was, but we can be sure that it was brightly-colored like that of tropical birds today.

Microraptor

Fossil finds Liaoning, China.

Name *Microraptor*, meaning "tiny hunter."

Time Early Cretaceous period, 130 – 125 million years ago.

Classification
Deinonychosaurs—dinosaurs with a killing claw on the hind foot. Microraptor is the smallest known of the coelurosaurs— meat-eating theropods with lightweight bones. Indeed it is the smallest known dinosaur.

Habitat Lakeside forests.

Physical characteristics
Very small meat-eating dinosaur, with feathered wings on both fore and hind legs.

TINY DINOSAUR

For 150 years we thought the chicken-sized meat-eating dinosaur *Compsognathus* was the smallest dinosaur known. That was before the discovery of *Microraptor* in lake deposits in China, and this turned out to be so small and lightweight that it could actually glide from tree to tree.

THE SMALLEST OF THE SMALL

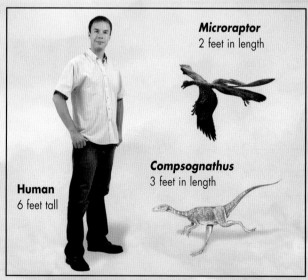

Human
6 feet tall

Microraptor
2 feet in length

Compsognathus
3 feet in length

This scale diagram shows you just how small dinosaurs could be! *Compsognathus* and *Microraptor* are two of the smallest discovered.

Lives of the Flying Reptiles

Pterosaurs
Their brightly colored crests would complement the dazzling plumage of today's birds.

But would these frightening and exotic creatures really survive in today's world?

Imagine if the skies were full of pterosaurs as well as birds. Just think of the mess! Fouled sidewalks. Terrified house pets. It would be rather beautiful too with flashes of intense color decorating our skies.

These creatures would be every bit as opportunistic as any other flying creature. The pterosaurs with spiky teeth would hunt for fish in modern oceans as easily as they hunted fish in the Mesozoic Era. Those with teeth adapted for feeding on ammonites would be poking about in rock pools, hunting mussels and clams. Those with beaks adapted for feeding on fruit would be flying in flocks around orchards and tree plantations.

The largest, those with wingspans comparable to those of small airplanes, are a bit of a mystery. Not enough is known about how they lived in the Mesozoic Era, and so it is unclear how they would fit into today's habitats. They certainly would not be swooping down, carrying off people, as we see in fantasy films—the basic laws of aerodynamics would prevent this.

The big question is, would they be able to compete with modern birds? For some reason, pterosaurs died out at the end of the Cretaceous period, while only three quarters of bird species were wiped out. It may be that the surviving birds were more resourceful and intelligent

than the pterosaurs, and better able to adapt to the changed conditions after the dinosaurs' extinction. If that is so, pterosaurs probably wouldn't be able to cope today.

Another matter that might prevent pterosaurs' assimilation into a modern habitat would be the atmosphere. Some scientists think that the mixture of gases in the air was different during the Mesozoic. It is possible that the level of either oxygen or carbon dioxide was higher than it is today. This would affect the air density and affect the ability of pterosaurs to fly. Larger-bodied flying animals, like *Quetzalcoatlus*, might have found it easier to lift off in a dense atmosphere, with more air for their wings to work against. A high oxygen level may also have meant a higher metabolic activity and an increased ability to tackle energetic actions like flying.

If the pterosaurs had adapted to fly in the particular atmosphere of Mesozoic times, they might not be able to do so today.

The lifestyle of a bird is different from that of a pterosaur. Birds build nests, lay hard-shelled eggs, hatch very immature young and spend a lot of time and energy looking after them and preparing them for adulthood. Pterosaurs, on the other hand, did not make complex nests. And we know from well-preserved egg fossils that the young hatched fully formed and ready for flight. They could look after themselves as soon as they were out of the egg—a useful advantage today.

Today, we combat nuisance birds with scarecrows, explosive bird scarers and protective nets. These would probably be effective against pterosaurs as well, but against the biggest, the protective nets would have to be far stronger than those we use against birds.

Pterosaur eggs
These leathery-shelled crocodile eggs are very similar to pterosaur eggs.

The End
of the Dinosaurs

For 160 million years the dinosaurs ruled the Earth. They expanded into all environments, on all continents. They developed into meat-eaters and plant-eaters. Their close relatives, the pterosaurs, took to the skies and the oceans were full of similarly gigantic creatures. Then suddenly they were all gone.

THEORY 1

So, what caused this abrupt disappearance? Scientists find it difficult to look so far back in time, to see what was going on then. For one thing, when we are talking about the history of the Earth the term "sudden" can actually mean a period of hundreds of thousands of years. In other words, dinosaurs might have vanished overnight, or they might have dwindled away, over what would be a long time to us.

Scientists would love to know whether the apparently sudden extinction of dinosaurs happened literally overnight, or over many thousands of years. Unfortunately it is impossible to date ancient rocks to the nearest day or year, or even thousand years. So the fossil record hasn't given us an answer yet.

If dinosaurs dwindled away, it might have been climate change or disease that killed them. Temperatures might have changed, causing new kinds of plants to grow. The plant-eating dinosaurs might not have been able to eat these plants and so starved to death, thereby interrupting the food chain and causing the deaths of other dinosaurs.

THEORY 2

If they disappeared quickly it would probably have been because of some great disaster. Perhaps there were widespread volcanic eruptions and earthquakes. Perhaps Earth was struck by a gigantic meteorite.

This last possibility, the gigantic meteorite, is considered the most likely by scientists today. If a huge mass of rock had struck Earth, the shock waves would have killed everything for hundreds of miles around.

It would have sent up such an enormous cloud of gas and dust into the atmosphere that the sun would have been blocked out for months or even years. Plants around the world would have died without the sunlight; plant-eating dinosaurs would have had nothing to eat and would therefore have died out; then the meat-eating dinosaurs would have had nothing to eat and they would also have died out. Eventually the skies would have cleared, and plants would have started growing again. But by then it would have been too late — the dinosaurs would be gone.

We can find compelling evidence that a meteorite struck Earth, when we look at layers of the planet that were formed 65 million years ago. We find minerals that are usually rare on the Earth's surface, but common in meteorites. These would have fallen as dust after a huge meteorite exploded when it hit the Earth. Rock fragments from this time show the kind of cracking and splintering that is caused by a massive explosion.

Finally, we think that we know where all this happened. Beneath the surface rocks of the Yucatán Peninsula in modern Mexico there is a huge buried crater called Chicxulub. This formed at exactly the time that the dinosaurs died out.

So, like detectives, we can put together the story of what happened at the end of the Age of Dinosaurs. A gigantic meteorite, the size of the Island of Manhattan, struck the Earth in the region of modern Mexico. The shock of the impact caused tsunamis to spread over nearby North and South America. The heat caused immediate forest fires. The shattered fragments of meteorite and Earth's crust formed a cloud that spread over the world. Combined, these factors led to the death of the dinosaurs and all the other spectacular reptiles of the time.

The Chicxulub Crater
65 million years ago a vast meteorite plunged through the atmosphere. It created a vast crater (top) in the region of the Yucatán Peninsula in Mexico. No sign of the crater remains on the surface today. Scientists think it is responsible for killing off the dinosaurs.

THE EVIDENCE

Chicxulub Impact Material
A lasting result of the meteorite impact was large quantities of disturbed material, as the Earth's crust was pulverised and the meteorite turned to dust. Not only was there shattered rock from the explosion, but seabeds were torn up by tsunamis and redeposited on land as jumbled masses of rock.

Layers
of Time

Millions of Years Ago

CENOZOIC ERA	
1.75	**QUATERNARY**
65	**TERTIARY**
MESOZOIC ERA	
145	**CRETACEOUS**
200	**JURASSIC**
251	**TRIASSIC**
295	**PERMIAN**
355	**CARBONIFEROUS**
PALAEOZOIC ERA	
410	**DEVONIAN**
435	**SILURIAN**
500	**ORDOVICIAN**
540	**CAMBRIAN**

3.4 BILLION YEARS AGO
Our first evidence of life is
from this time.

PRECAMBRIAN

ERA

4 BILLION YEARS AGO
Earth's crust begins to form.

PERIOD

Dinosaurs lived 65 million years ago. We know about them not only by studying their fossilized remains, but by studying the rocks in which they are found. Scientists can read the layers of the rocks like a book, telling what the landscape and climate conditions were like all those years ago; what animal life existed in times gone past; and when all this happened.

TIME

Geological history covers an immense stretch of time. So immense that we can hardly imagine it. We are talking about millions of years, hundreds of millions of years, thousands of millions of years… To make it easy, scientists don't think in terms of numbers of years. They divide Earth's history up into manageable chunks called eras and periods.

The Age of Dinosaurs is the Mesozoic Era, and that is divided into the Triassic, the Jurassic and the Cretaceous periods. This stretch of time began 251 million years ago and ended 65 million years ago. The dinosaurs appeared towards the end of the Triassic period.

So, dinosaurs might have only been extinct for 65 million years, but before that they ruled the Earth for 160 million years —about three times as long. That is about 640 times as long as *Homo sapiens*!

STRATIGRAPHY

Our knowledge of dinosaurs comes from the fossils we find in rocks. If you look at a sequence of sedimentary rock, (rock that has formed from sands and muds), you will see that it is in layers. The layers are called beds or strata. Sorting out the sequences of rocks is a very careful process. It involves a science called stratigraphy. A stratigrapher can read these layers and work out the history of the rocks.

For example, a layer of sandstone may show where a sandbank once stood at a river's mouth. Above this there may be a layer of limestone. The limestone would have formed from limy mud at the bottom of the sea, and so this shows that the sea flooded over the sandbank. Above this there may be a layer of shale which forms from mud. So this may show where mud from a tributary river flowed in.

Rock sequences

These are never completely continuous which is why it's difficult for stratigraphers to read them. If the original sediments are raised above the surface of the water, they erode away. Then they may sink again and new sediments will form on the eroded surface.

The oldest rocks lie at the bottom of a sequence and the younger rocks are deposited on top. So when we see a geological time scale (like the one on the left) printed in a book, the oldest period is shown at the bottom and the youngest at the top to reflect this.

The beds in one outcrop of rock may look so distinctive that they can be identified in another outcrop some distance off. These beds would have once been continuous but those in between the outcrops have since eroded away.

The fossils contained in the rocks tell the real story. Different animals lived in different periods. So, if we can identify the animal fossils in a rock we can usually tell how old the rocks are. Also, different animals lived in different environments. For example it may be difficult to tell a shale that was formed from mud deposited in a river, from one that was formed from mud deposited at the bottom of the sea. But, if we find the fossils of freshwater snails in it, we know that it formed from river mud.

Clues like these help us to understand the history of dinosaurs and the world in which they lived.

SEDIMENTARY ROCK SEQUENCE

Coal
frequently contains fossilized tree stumps.

Shale
is made up of mud particles.

Limestone
contains many fossils, including ones like this crinoid.

Sandstone
contains many fossils—like this footprint.

Dinosaur
Discoveries

Where?

Since the first dinosaur remains were found, in England in the 1820s, dinosaur discoveries have been made all over the world. In the beginning scientists used hammers and chisels to find them. Today they sometimes use computers and satellites, but nothing beats a sharp eye!

19th Century
The most important phase of early dinosaur discovery happened in America, in the second half of the 19th century. Scientists from universities and museums on the east coast followed the settlers west and started finding skeletons. They were so jealous of each other's finds that they started to compete, to unearth the most and the best. This period is called the "bone wars" and resulted in about 150 different types of dinosaur being discovered by 1900.

20th Century
From then on people started to actively look for, and discover, dinosaur fossils all over the world. German and British teams

found them in Africa; expeditions from America discovered important remains in the Gobi Desert in Mongolia; and sheep farmers turned them up in Australia. Eventually, in the 1970s, dinosaur fossils were even being found in the wilderness of Antarctica.

Montana, America, 1897
The classic late Cretaceous dinosaur site.

Africa, 1984
Sir David Attenborough with sauropod bones.

21st Century
Today sites are being revisited and studied with more modern techniques. Thanks to these, even greater discoveries are now being made, including dinosaurs with fossilized soft parts. More careful excavation techniques are revealing details like stomach contents that older, rougher methods overlooked. More attention is being paid to fossils like footprints, that tell us not so much about an ancient animal's appearance, but its lifestyle and social life.

England, 2004
Fossilized footprint thought to belong to an Iguanodon.

How?

Most dinosaur finds are accidents. Scientists aiming to find a dinosaur skeleton are faced with a difficult task. They have to find rocks that date back to dinosaur times and that are from environments in which dinosaurs lived. This is hard because over the years rocks have moved with the continents. You could find a prehistoric riverside rock in a desert environment today. When searching a vast open area, such as the Gobi Desert in Mongolia, that is a huge space to look for a particular rock type.

There are many tools to help scientists. A new one for the dinosaur hunter exploring areas like Mongolia, is satellite photography. Scientists analyze the pattern of light waves reflected from Earth and photographed by satellite. Different rocks reflect light in different ways and scientists may recognize potentially fossil-bearing rocks from this. A huge area can be photographed, and from the results scientists can focus their ground search.

There are also machines that use radar technology to look deep inside rocks. Scientists use it to see what is buried below and plan an excavation.

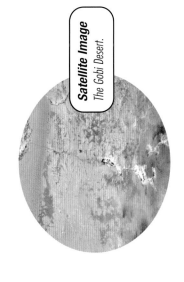

Satellite Image
The Gobi Desert.

Ground-penetrating Radar
This allows scientists to see inside Earth.

Another method of finding fossils is to set an explosion at the Earth's surface. This sends shock waves through the rock which bounce off things buried in them. Different patterns of waves come back, straight ones for rocks and irregular ones for fossils.

Most minerals, and therefore some dinosaur fossils are slightly radioactive. Sensitive instruments can detect this at the Earth's surface. As fossils are made of different minerals to the surrounding rocks, there may be a difference in radioactivity. This method has only been used in a couple of cases to date.

Magnetometry
These machines pick up radioactive waves from fossils.

Could this be you?

It is difficult to know where the next great dinosaur find is going to be. Currently we know of about 500 different dinosaur types. This could represent anything from a third to a fifth of all the dinosaurs that ever lived. There are many more unknown kinds of dinosaurs out there, in the rocks, waiting for the next generation of palaeontologists to discover them, dig them up and add to our knowledge of dinosaur life.

Saichania
Found in the Gobi Desert.

Changing
Planet

The continents are moving constantly, through a process called "plate tectonics." The Earth has always been like this, it happened during the 160 million year reign of the dinosaurs and it is happening today. The Atlantic Ocean is 98 feet wider now than it was when Christopher Columbus crossed it 500 years ago!

SUPERCONTINENT

If we look at a map of the Earth as it was at the beginning of the Age of Dinosaurs, we see something unusual. All the continents are clumped together as one single landmass. They had been moving around for about four billion years before that. But during the Triassic period, they all happened to collide together. The result was one supercontinent that we call Pangaea. Dinosaurs developed on Pangaea, and spread across the landmass. They concentrated around the coast, because the heart of the supercontinent consisted of searing desert. We know this because we often find fossils of Triassic dinosaurs around the edges of the continents.

Fossils prove that the same kinds of dinosaurs existed across the whole of the supercontinent from one side to the other. Modern South Africa represents the southern edge of Pangaea. In South Africa we find the remains of long-necked plant-eating dinosaurs, which are very similar to the long-necked plant-eaters we find in Germany—the northern edge of Pangaea. Small meat-eating dinosaurs from South and East Africa are similar to those in Arizona—which were the eastern and western corners of Pangaea.

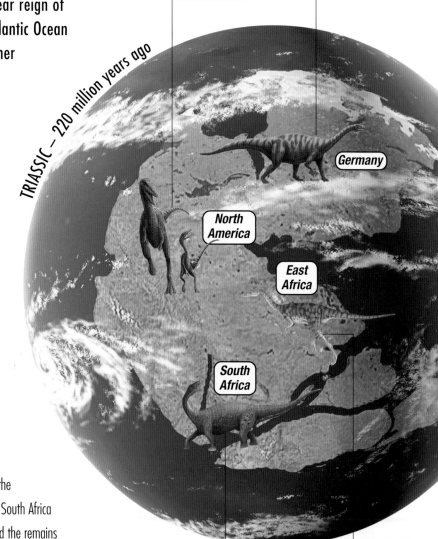

TRIASSIC – 220 million years ago

Coelophysis
A small active theropod that hunted along the watercourses of North America.

Plateosaurus
A prosauropod that fed on the oasis plants of the dry German Triassic plains.

Germany

North America

East Africa

South Africa

Euskelosaurus
A South African prosauropod that had a similar appearance and lifestyle to Plateosaurus from Germany.

Syntarsus
An East African theropod that was almost identical to Coelophysis from North America.

MODERN · CONTINENT

As time went on Pangaea split up. Cracks appeared and the landmass broke into sections and began to drift apart. By the end of the Cretaceous period—the end of the Age of Dinosaurs—these sections had formed the modern continents and were separate from one another. The original dinosaurs that lived on these sections had been adapting in their own ways.

By the end of the Cretaceous period there were different dinosaurs in North America to those in South America, and different dinosaurs in Europe and Asia from those in Africa.

Since the end of the Cretaceous period the continents have continued to drift. What would have happened if the meteorite had missed? What if the dinosaurs had not become extinct 65 million years ago? Would they have continued unchanged until the present day, as we have shown in this book? If the dinosaurs had continued to exist until today, they might be even more different. They might have continued to adapt at different rates and in different directions, separated by the different continents.

Sauropelta
The armored dinosaurs mostly lived in North America and Asia.

Tarbosaurus
The tyrannosaurids were the big meat-eaters of the northern hemisphere.

CRETACEOUS – 100 million years ago

Mongolia

North America

Africa

South America

Carcharodontosaurus
The big meat-eaters of the southern continents were the carnosaurs.

Saltasaurus
Sauropods continued to thrive in South America but were dying out elsewhere.

Changing
World

Not only did the positions of the continents change while the dinosaurs were rulers of the Earth, climates changed too. Most importantly, plants changed as well. All of this affected the rise of the dinosaurs.

Cycad

Triassic

The first dinosaurs in the Triassic period lived by the seaside, along river banks and in desert oases. These were places where water was plentiful. The vegetation was different from that found today. The undergrowth consisted mostly of horsetails, ferns and bush-sized cycads. These are still found in hot dry places, such as deserts. The trees that existed then were mostly conifers, of the kind that we now only see in the mountains of South America.

The first plant-eating dinosaurs adapted to feed on these plants. And the plants adapted along with them. The main type of conifer developed hard sword-like needles to discourage the early herbivores from eating them.

Plateosaurus
The first plant-eating dinosaurs belonged to the prosauropod group. Plateosaurus is a typical prosauropod. It had a long neck, small head and a big body which contained its massive digestive gut.

Brachiosaurus
The long-necked sauropods of the Jurassic period could feed on both undergrowth and the tops of high trees.

Jurassic

In the Jurassic period the climates became milder and moister. Pangaea began to break up. Shallow seas spread over the edges of the continents. The vegetation still consisted of ferns and horsetails, cycads and conifers. But now forests were much more widespread and the dinosaurs flourished. New and increased vegetation encouraged the growth of big plant-eating dinosaurs and subsequently meat-eaters.

Magnolia

Triceratops
The narrow beaks of the Cretaceous horned dinosaurs allowed them to select the best bits from the new flowering plants.

Cretaceous

Come the Cretaceous period vegetation began to change. Until then plants reproduced by spores, with millions of spores being released and fertilized in a hit-or-miss process. The resulting plants grew slowly. As soon as they started to grow they were eaten by dinosaurs, and did not have a chance to reproduce.

Then a major new group of plants appeared, the angiosperms, or flowering plants. This new group was a rare first, they produced seeds. Seeds could lie quietly until the time was right, and then germinate into plants that grew quickly before they could be eaten. The new flowering plants were hugely successful and took over in many parts of the world, and the dinosaurs had to adapt themselves to eating these new kinds of plants.

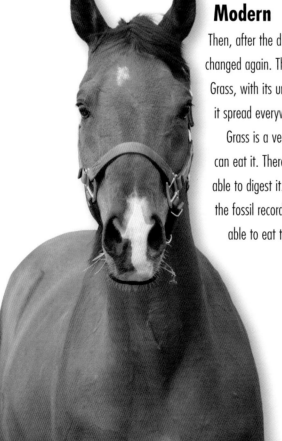

Modern

Then, after the dinosaurs all died out at the end of the Cretaceous period, the vegetation changed again. The climates became cooler and drier, and the forests began to die back. Grass, with its underground stems, was good at surviving these new conditions — it spread everywhere.

Grass is a very tough plant, and only very specialized animals like cows and horses, can eat it. There were no grasslands in dinosaur times, and there were no dinosaurs able to digest it. This is one of the main reasons that the dinosaurs we know from the fossil record would not really be able to survive today — they would not be able to eat the kinds of plants we have now.

Horse
Modern grass-eaters have very strong teeth and complex digestive systems to eat and break down tough grass leaves.

Modern Grass

Changing
Life

Animal life does not stay the same forever. It changes and adapts to different conditions. It has done so for as long as there has been life on Earth. The dinosaurs went through periods of change like this, developing and adapting as the Age of Dinosaurs went on.

Life, in one form or another, has existed ever since the surface of the Earth was cool enough and moist enough to support it. The earliest living things were probably no more than cells that could absorb raw materials from around them, and reproduce themselves. But from such humble beginnings the history of life developed.

Then, a little over 500 million years ago, at the beginning of the Cambrian period, a great change took place. Hard shells suddenly appeared, with calcite shells in mollusks and other seashell-type animals, and chitin shells in crab-like arthropods. These shells made good fossils after their owners died. From then on the fossil record has been rich and informative.

The next great advance was the hard-shelled egg. This could be laid on land, and at this stage reptiles appeared.

Bacteria

Jellyfish

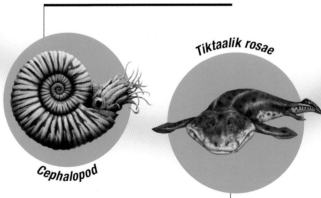

Cephalopod

Tiktaalik rosae

Westlothiana

By far the greatest part of Earth's history is contained in the time period that we call the Precambrian. During this time, (about seven-eighths of the time that Earth has existed), living things adapted quietly in the ocean. All animal life in this period consisted of small, soft-bodied animals that hardly ever fossilized.

One group of early animals developed a bony skeleton, and so fish developed. But it was not long before fish ventured out of the water. Adaptations for this included the ability to breathe air, and specialized limbs that allowed them to crawl over land. They became amphibians. However, these amphibians were only half-way to becoming fully land-living animals. They still had to return to water to breed and to lay eggs.

Dinosaurs took over as the main reptile group after the mammal-like reptiles declined. The fact that the dinosaurs were so successful meant that mammals remained small because they had not the space or opportunity to change much.

Had the dinosaurs not died out, then we would not see the vast range of mammals that exist today. If there is a gap to be exploited then nature will always adapt to fill it. The extinction of the dinosaurs left a wide range of gaps that survivors could adapt into, and the mammals were the most suitable animals for doing so.

Ouranosaurus

Dimetrodon

Eoraptor

The advantage dinosaurs had over other reptiles lay in the arrangement of their legs and hips. Dinosaurs were able to stand with their legs held beneath them, like big mammals do, not splayed out at the side like lizards and crocodiles. The weight of their body was carried at the tops of their legs rather than slung between them. Two lines of dinosaurs emerged:

All kinds of reptile lines developed in the Permian period. The most important in early times was a group we call the mammal-like reptiles. These flourished at first, then almost all died out, but those that survived adapted to the changing conditions on Earth and became mammals.

The first were the "lizard-hipped dinosaurs," so called because the bones of their hips were arranged like those of a lizard (even though their legs weren't). They were the meat-eating dinosaurs and long-necked plant-eaters. The meat-eaters were swift and two-footed. The plant-eaters were much slower and went on all fours, to better support the great weight of their big digestive systems.

The other line consisted of the "bird-hipped dinosaurs." These were all plant-eaters. The bird-like arrangement of hip bones meant that the heavy digestive system could be carried between the legs, rather than in front of the hips. This meant they were able to balance on their hind legs. Some, however, were covered in armor or plates, or had large horned heads.

These were too heavy for a two-footed existence and they went around on all fours.

Today's
Dinosaurs

Dinosaurs have survived to the present day—but in a completely different form. It is now widely accepted that birds are living dinosaurs because they are so closely related. Birds descended from meat-eating dinosaurs back in the Jurassic period, and managed to survive the extinction at the end of the Cretaceous.

Look at the earliest bird that we know, *Archaeopteryx*. It is certainly a bird, as it has wings and feathers. But it also has dinosaur features. It does not have a beak, but has jaws and teeth instead—just like a dinosaur. Its wings have three clawed fingers on the hands—just like a dinosaur. It has a long bony tail—just like a dinosaur. It seems evident that it has descended from the small meat-eating dinosaurs of the time.

Archaeopteryx
The first bird still retained many dinosaur features.

Since then birds have adapted into the specialized flying animals that we know today. They have lightweight beaks rather than teeth, to keep their overall weight down. They have compact bodies with the bones fused together, to give strong support to the wing muscles. They have short stumpy tails with a fan of feathers, to help with steering. In fact birds look nothing like what we would imagine a dinosaur to. Yet it seems clear that they descended from them.

The dinosaurs of the Cretaceous period shared their world with birds that we would recognize today. Shortly after *Archaeopteryx* there lived many kinds of birds that looked more like modern species.

Wings
The layout of the feathers of a modern bird are just like those of Archaeopteryx.

Skeleton
The skeleton of a modern bird is more compact than that of its ancestor.

Tail
The fan of feathers replaces the long bony dinosaur-like tail.

Beak
A modern bird weighs less because it has a beak instead of a toothy jaw.

At the end of the Cretaceous period most of the bird families became extinct, along with the dinosaurs. However, enough of them survived to continue to present times.

Soon after the dinosaurs died out, mammals spread everywhere. At first there were no big meat-eating mammals. But the plant-eating mammals were a good source of food, and so something was bound to adapt to eat them. It was the birds that became the big meat-eaters.

Huge flightless birds, taller than you are, stalked the Earth. With their long hind legs, stumpy forelimbs, flexible necks and big fierce heads, they looked just like their ancestors, the meat-eating dinosaurs. However they had huge curved beaks, (bigger and stronger even than those of eagles), with which they killed and ripped up the mammals on which they fed.

There is nothing like these monster birds living now. Their places on Earth were eventually taken by meat-eating mammals like lions and wolves. Birds continued to change into the shapes they are today.

So, perhaps we can say that dinosaurs did not die out. They changed as Earth's conditions changed; and survived by growing extreme adaptations.

Dinosaurs did not become extinct — it seems they just grew wings and flew away!

Phorusrhacos
This killer bird of the early Tertiary period looked and acted just like one of the meat-eating dinosaurs it replaced.

83

What If...?

What defines a dinosaur?

A» The arrangement of bones in the hip, and the shape of the leg bones. These allow it to walk on straight legs, held beneath it like a mammal.

Why is a dinosaur called a dinosaur?

A» The word "Dinosauria" was invented by British anatomist, Sir Richard Owen, when he gave a talk in 1842. It means "terrible lizard" and was invented to describe the only three dinosaurs known at that time — Megalosaurus, Iguanodon and Hylaeosaurus.

Sir Richard Owen

Q Are there any dinosaurs alive today?

No. Unless you count birds. Many scientists think that birds should be called dinosaurs because they are so closely related. These scientists call the animals that we would regard as dinosaurs "non-avian dinosaurs" to distinguish them from birds, or "avian dinosaurs."

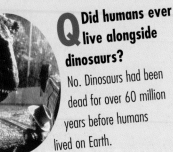

Q Did humans ever live alongside dinosaurs?

No. Dinosaurs had been dead for over 60 million years before humans lived on Earth.

Q Could we bring dinosaurs to life from their fossilized DNA?

No. This makes a good story but it is not good science. There is no way that DNA (the building blocks of all creatures) can survive intact over tens of millions of years.

Q If dinosaurs suddenly appeared today, how would we look after them?

In a very big zoo! Most of the dinosaurs were very large. The bigger an animal is, the bigger the area it needs to live in. We would also need vast farms to produce enough food to keep these captive dinosaurs alive. Likewise, a big meat-eater would need to be fed big quantities of meat.

Q Is it at all possible that a few dinosaurs might have survived in a remote corner of the world, where nobody has been?

A big dinosaur would need a very big area of land to support it. We would have discovered such a big area of land by now.

Is the Loch Ness Monster a dinosaur?

A»

Definitely not. There were no dinosaurs that lived in the water like this. If the question was "Is the Loch Ness Monster a plesiosaur?" that would be different. A plesiosaur was a reptile that was well adapted to life in the water—streamlined body, paddle limbs, streamlined head. If the Loch Ness Monster exists, it may well have these features that would allow it to live in the water. But that would not necessarily mean that it is a plesiosaur.

Q Could we have kept any dinosaurs as pets?

Small feathered dinosaurs, such as *Archaeopteryx*, would make good pets. They would probably need the same amount of care as exotic birds, like parrots.

Q If dinosaurs had not died out 65 million years ago, would mammals be here?

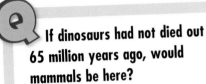

No. Mammals are only here because there are no dinosaurs. In the Age of Dinosaurs mammals were small mouse-like or opossum-like ones. There wasn't enough room for them so they did not grow much larger than a cat or dog. All the habitats were occupied by dinosaurs and other big reptiles.

Only when the dinosaurs died out did mammals have room to expand. With no plant-eating dinosaurs to compete against, mammals were able to develop into large herbivores. With no meat-eating dinosaurs around, new meat-eating animals developed —first giant flightless birds, and then carnivorous mammals. This could not have happened if dinosaurs were still the dominant animal type. So it is because dinosaurs died out that mammals exist.

Q Is it true that a rhinoceros is descended from a *Triceratops*?

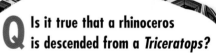

No. They are quite different animals. They do look like one another, though, with their big bodies and their horns. This is because although they are separated by millions of years, they have the same lifestyle, and have similar shapes to be able to cope with it. Both have thick hides to defend themselves against predators, and horns for fighting and display.

Q If they were alive today, would dinosaurs survive in our environment?

If they had enough of the right things to eat, they probably would. Meat-eaters would be quite successful. But plant-eaters would find it more difficult because they were selective about what they ate. Coniferous forests would be best for most of them.

What About...?

How tall is the tallest dinosaur?
A» Possibly the *Sauroposeidon*. Only four neck bones have ever been found, by analyzing those and the proportions of the closely related *Brachiosaurus* we can deduce that it was over about 60 feet high.

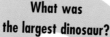

What was the largest dinosaur?
The heaviest was probably *Argentinosaurus*. It would have weighed 90 to 115 tons.

What size is the biggest dinosaur footprint?
Big sauropod footprints found recently in Australia are well over three feet long. But it is impossible to say what dinosaur made them.

Dino dung... phew!

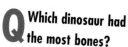

Which dinosaur had the most bones?
Dinosaurs all had pretty much the same number of bones (just as cats, dogs and horses do), but they differ a little by the number of vertebrae in the tail.

What is the average size of dino dung?
Scientists call fossilized dino dung 'coprolite'. It is very important in telling us what the dinosaurs were eating. It's usually hard to find complete poops of herbivores, they tended to get broken up and scattered. They were probably like monster cow plops, covering many feet. Meat-eater poops are like those of dogs and cats—more compact. Paleontologists have found a three-foot long *T. rex* coprolite full of *Triceratops* bones.

How small was the smallest dinosaur?
The smallest we know is *Microraptor* at 2.5 feet long, light enough to glide between trees.

How long was the longest neck of a dinosaur?
The sauropod *Erketu* has the longest neck in relation to its body—24 feet compared with the body that was 12 feet long—we do not know how long the tail was so we don't know the length of the whole animal. The longest overall was *Mamenchisaurus* that had a total length of 90 feet and a neck that was 32 feet long.

What was the fastest dinosaur?
The fastest runners would have been the ostrich mimics, like *Ornithomimus*. They probably ran at speeds of 25 miles per hour. There were no swimming dinosaurs or flying dinosaurs (unless you count gliding *Microraptor*).

What was the most blood-thirsty dinosaur?
Small meat-eaters would have to be very fierce if they were to kill something much bigger than themselves, so probably *Velociraptor* would qualify.

What was the most powerful dinosaur?
Probably the biggest sauropods, like *Argentinosaurus* or *Sauroposeidon*. They would have to be powerful to move their great weights around.

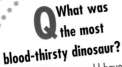

Q» Which dinosaur has the longest tail? **A»** The longest complete tail that we know i

Tyrannosaurus

Q If a *Tyrannosaurus* fought a *Spinosaurus,* which would win?
That is impossible to answer. They did not live at the same time or in the same place and would never have met. Each of these animals was adapted to a particular landscape and hunted a particular prey. If, by some magic chance, they did meet one another they would not know what to do. Neither would see the other as prey or predator. They would probably ignore each other and not get into a fight.

Q How many bones did a *Tyrannosaurus* have?
We don't know. We have never found a complete skeleton.

Q How many teeth did a *Tyrannosaurus* have?
About 50.

Q Is it true or false that chickens are related to *Tyrannosaurus*?
In that it is true that all meat-eating dinosaurs are related to modern birds, then it is true.

Q How many *Tyrannosaurus* could you fit into Yankee Stadium?
Only one. Like a lion or any other hunter, it would guard its territory jealously. Any other Tyrannosaurs that came close would be attacked.

Q What was a *Tyrannosaur's* life span?
About 30 years.

Diplodocus, with a length of 45 feet. We know of bigger animals such as Seismosaurus and Supersaurus, but we do not have complete tails for these that we can measure.

What Were They Really Like...?

Eyes

Q **Did dinosaurs have slit eyes?**
Perhaps. If the active meat-eaters hunted like modern cats, they would probably have had slit eyes like cats too.

Q **How far could a dinosaur see?**
It depends. Hunting dinosaurs would have needed sharp eyesight to keep their prey in view. In some their eyes were pointed forward like ours, to help them to judge the distance to their prey. Plant-eaters would have been better off with eyes that could see around as far as possible, to detect danger coming from every direction.

Q **Were any dinosaurs nocturnal?**
Some probably were. *Troodon* and its relatives had very large eyes. This has been taken as an indication that it hunted owl-like at night. Small plant-eating *Leaellynasaura* lived within the Antarctic Circle, where the nights would have lasted for months. It must have been able to forage in the dark.

Male/Female

Q **How do you differentiate between female and male dinosaurs?**
Sometimes we can tell the difference by the shape of the hip bones. Often in a fossilized dinosaur herd we find two different sizes of adults. In this instance, the larger forms are usually the females and the smaller the males. The females were larger because they produced large broods of eggs.

Q **Was the pack leader usually female or male?**
As in most of today's packs, it would have been male.

Teeth

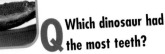

Q **Which dinosaur had the most teeth?**
Duck-billed dinosaurs such as *Edmontosaurus* had literally hundreds of teeth in their jaw. However, a lot of these were not being used at the same time. Most were growing upwards to replace those that were being worn away through use.

Why do some dinosaurs have lots of small teeth, and some not very many big teeth?
It depended on what they ate and what job the teeth had to do. A meat-eater like *Tyrannosaurus* had jaws that worked best when the teeth were in a line, like the teeth of a saw. Plant-eating prosauropods like *Plateosaurus* had teeth that slightly overlapped along the jaw, allowing them to rip away at plant material like vegetable graters.

Which dinosaur had the biggest teeth?
The biggest teeth found so far belong to *Giganotosaurus* and these are about 6 inches long. Our picture is life-size!

Function

Q **What color was a dinosaur's blood?**

It would probably have contained the same chemicals as the blood of modern animals, and so it would have been the same rich red color.

Q **How far could a dinosaur travel without resting?** Many of the big plant-eating dinosaurs seem to have migrated hundreds of miles with the seasons.

Q **How did dinosaurs fight?** With teeth, with horns, with spikes, with tail clubs, with claws—with whatever they had!

Q **Were any dinosaurs renowned for their brilliant camouflage?**

As we don't know what color the dinosaurs were we cannot answer that question. However, it seems likely that hunting dinosaurs could see in color in order to differentiate their prey, and so the plant-eaters were probably camouflaged.

Q **How would a long neck help a dinosaur?** Like the hose of a vacuum cleaner, it would reach around without having to move its big heavy body.

Q **What kind of skin did most dinosaurs have?** Fossilized skin is hardly ever found, but when it is we can see that it usually consisted of flat scales—not overlapping like on a fish but abutting, like a lizard's. Sometimes there were bony lumps set into the skin, and these would be covered in horn. Some small meat-eating dinosaurs were covered in feathers instead.

Birth & Death

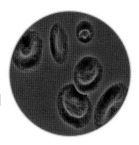

Q **Did dinosaurs give birth to live young or lay eggs?**

We know of plenty of dinosaur eggs and nests—enough to tell us that most of them laid eggs. However, the pachycephalosaurs had very wide hips, which would suggest that they gave birth to live young.

Q **How quickly did dinosaurs grow from baby to adult?**

Small meat-eaters like *Troodon* probably took 3 to 5 years to reach adulthood. The prosauropod *Massospondylus* took about 15 years. A big sauropod like *Bothriospopndylus* seems to have taken 43 years to grow to an adult. Most thorough work has been done on *Tyrannosaurus*. It grew slowly until it was about 14 years old. Then it grew quickly until it reached its adult size at 18, and died by 30.

Q **Were there any diseases that could kill dinosaurs?** There must have been. We find deformities in bones that were obviously caused by disease (the nodule on these bones is a tumor). There is even a theory that the dinosaurs became extinct because migrating dinosaurs spread diseases to others.

Q **Were prehistoric parasites more deadly than modern parasites?** The thing about parasites is that they only attack a specific host. So parasites in dinosaur times would have been as deadly to them as ours are to us.

Q **How long was the lifespan of the average dinosaur?**

It varied. Small meat-eaters were probably quite short-lived. Large meat-eaters like *Tyrannosaurus* lived to be about 30. The big sauropods may have lived to be over 100. However, life was hard in dinosaur times, and it would have been rare for a dinosaur to live long.

Q **What dinosaur lived the longest and to how old?**

The big sauropods were the long-lived ones, but just how long they lived would have depended on whether they were warm-blooded or cold-blooded. If they were warm-blooded they may have lived to 120 years. If they were cold-blooded they may have survived to 200 years. Cold-blooded animals have slower metabolic rates and their life processes occur more slowly. Therefore they tend to live longer.

Do You Know...?

Ankylosaurus

Q Did all dinosaurs live at the same time?

No. The first dinosaurs were quite primitive types. As time went on they developed into different shapes and sizes. Some groups of dinosaurs died out early in the Age of Dinosaurs—such as stegosaurs. These were replaced by other kinds of dinosaurs— in this case *Ankylosaurus* which lived 75 million years after *Stegosaurus*.

Stegosaurus

Q Can we tell what color the dinosaurs were?

Skin color never fossilizes. But we can make comparisons with modern animals. We look at what color scheme works for a modern animal with a particular lifestyle in a particular environment. Then we can be confident that this color scheme would have worked for a prehistoric animal in a similar environment. So we can guess that meat-eating dinosaurs may have been striped or spotted like meat-eating tigers and leopards. Very big plant-eating dinosaurs may have been a dull gray like elephants.

Q Were dinosaurs the same all over the world?

No. At the beginning of the Age of Dinosaurs there were similar kinds of dinosaurs living in different places. But as the Age of Dinosaurs went on, different types began to emerge in different places. This was especially true when the supercontinent of Pangaea, that existed during the Triassic period, broke up in the Jurassic. Then in the Cretaceous period the individual continents spread apart. Different dinosaur types began to thrive on the different continents.

Q Are we sure that the dinosaurs really looked like how we show them?

That is difficult to answer! Our view of what dinosaurs looked like is changing all the time. When the first dinosaur bones were found, no-one had any idea of what dinosaurs looked like. The bones obviously came from some big reptile, and so early scientists imagined that they were like giant lizards. For example, the first drawing of an *Iguanodon* looked like a gigantic iguana lizard. (1)

A little later, they realized that dinosaur leg bones did not stick out at the sides, like a lizard's, but were upright, supporting the body like pillars. So then scientists thought that dinosaurs looked more like mammals, that have straight legs. Imagine an *Iguanodon* that looked like a rhinoceros. (2)

Then whole articulated skeletons began to be discovered. For the first time scientists could see the shape of the whole animal. Drawings of *Iguanodon* from that time made it look like a kangaroo, sitting back on its hind legs and supported by its tail. (3)

Today we think that *Iguanodon* was actually a four-footed animal, that walked with its tail in the air. We might find out something else soon, and there will be new and different pictures of what *Iguanodon* looked like. (4)

(1)

(2)

(3)

(4)

(3)
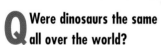

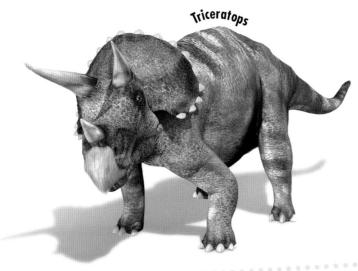

Triceratops

Species

Q What is the most common dinosaur known?

There are fossil beds of horned dinosaurs like *Triceratops* that consist of over a thousand individuals. That is an enormous herd! They are the most common that we know about.

How many known species of dinosaurs were there?

We know of over 500 but more are being found all the time.

Q What was on Earth before dinosaurs?

All sorts of things—insects, shellfish, amphibians, reptiles—in fact all the kinds of animals that we have today, except for birds. They did not develop until half way through the Age of Dinosaurs.

Tyrannosaurus

First & Last

Q What were the first and last dinosaurs to live on the face of the Earth?

The earliest one that we know about was *Eoraptor*—a small meat-eater from the late Triassic of South America. At the end of the Cretaceous period all the dinosaurs that still existed died out together—so it's hard to say what was the last. We do know that they included *Tyrannosaurus*, *Ankylosaurus* and *Triceratops*.

Coelacanth

Eoraptor

Discoveries

Q Which was the first dinosaur to be discovered?
Megalosaurus.

Q Which place is most popular for finding fossils?
The American mid-west, states like Wyoming, Colorado and Montana.

Q Where are you most likely to find dinosaur bones?
Where you find rocks that formed in dinosaur times from deposits laid down in lakes, riverbeds and deserts.

Q What is the oldest fossil recorded?
Probably fossilized bacteria, three-and-a-half billion years old.

Q Will all the dinosaur fossils ever be discovered?
No. The vast majority of them are buried deep in the Earth. We will only ever be able to find the ones that lie near the surface.

Are there any more dinosaurs yet to be found?
Yes. We're sure that only a fraction of those that ever existed have been discovered. There will be many more buried in remote corners of the world.

Glossary

Altitude The height of something, especially above sea level.

Ammonite An extinct marine mollusk with a flat-coiled spiral shell, found as fossils chiefly in Jurassic and Cretaceous deposits.

Amphibians Animals that are able to live on both land and water.

Arthropod An invertebrate animal that has a shell and jointed limbs, like insects, spiders, and crustaceans.

Archaeology The study of human history and prehistory through the excavation of sites and the analysis of physical remains.

Arid Having little or no rain; dry and barren.

Atmosphere The layer of enveloping gases which surround the Earth.

Avian Relating or related to birds.

Bacteria Microscopic organisms that can cause disease.

Baleen The bony flexible strips in the upper jaws of whales that feed by filtering food from the ocean water.

Biped An animal which walks on two feet.

Calcite A white or colorless mineral.

Carnivore An animal that feeds on meat.

Carrion The decaying flesh of a dead animal.

Cephalopod Literally the "head-footed" animals. The modern types, the octopus and squid, appear to have legs branching from their faces.

Ceratopsian dinosaur A type of dinosaur that had frills, spikes, and horns as protection.

Chitin A hard, semi-transparent material found throughout the natural world.

Coal A combustible black rock consisting mainly of carbonized plant matter and used as fuel.

Conifer A tree bearing cones and evergreen needle-like or scale-like leaves.

Continent Any of the world's main continuous expanses of land, usually consisting of an ancient core and surrounded by successively younger mountain ranges.

Creodont A carnivorous mammal of the Early Tertiary period.

Crystal A piece of a solid substance having a natural geometrically regular form with symmetrically arranged faces.

Cycad A tall, palm-like plant that can be found in tropical regions.

Duckbill A type of dinosaur that had a beak similar to a duck's beak or bill.

Eon The largest division of geological time. It comprises several eras.

Equator An imaginary line that divides the Earth into a northern hemisphere and a southern hemisphere.

Era A division of geological time. Typically an era lasts for hundreds of millions of years, and covers several periods. For example the Mesozoic Era comprises the Triassic, Jurassic, and Cretaceous periods.

Erosion A gradual wearing away of rocks or soil.

Excavation The careful removal of dirt from an area in order to find buried remains.

Fauna The animals of a particular region, habitat, or geological period.

Fern A flowerless plant which has feathery or leafy fronds.

Flora The plants of a particular region, habitat, or geological period.

Fossil The remains or impression of a prehistoric plant or animal embedded in rock and preserved.

Geology The study of the Earth, how it is made and how it has changed.

Glaciated Covered or having been covered by glaciers or ice sheets.

Herbivore An animal which eats only plants.

Hominid The group of animals to which humans belong.

Horsetail A flowerless plant with a hollow jointed stem.

Ice Age A period of time when climates were cooler than they are now and glaciers were more extensive.

Ichthyosaur One of a group of swimming reptiles from the Mesozoic. They had streamlined fish-like bodies and tail fins.

Incubate To hatch eggs by keeping them warm.

Invertebrate An animal without a backbone.

Juvenile Young, not yet adult.

Landmass A continent or other large body of land.

Latitude The angular distance of a place north or south of the Equator.

Maneuverability Capable of being moved.

Marginocephalians A group of dinosaurs with armored heads. They consisted of the pachycephalosaurids, like *Stygimoloch*, and the ceratopsians, like *Triceratops*.

Mass extinction An event that brings about the extinction of a large number of animals and plants. There have been about five mass extinctions in the history of life on Earth.

Membrane A thin skin or similar covering.

Meteorite A piece of rock from space.

Mineral A naturally-formed inorganic substance with a specific chemical composition. Minerals are the building blocks of rocks.

Molecule A group of atoms bonded together.

Mosasaur A member of a group of big swimming reptiles of the Cretaceous period, closely related to modern monitor lizards.

Nocturnal Active at night.

Oases Green areas in a desert, where there is water and plants grow.

Open plains Wide spaces without trees.

Organism An individual animal, plant, or single-celled life form.

Ornithischian A beaked, herbivorous dinosaur which roamed in herds.

Ornithopod A kind of bipedal plant-eating dinosaur which lived during the Late Triassic, Jurassic, and Cretacious periods.

Palaeo- As a prefix this means something ancient.

Palaeontology The study of ancient life and fossils.

Period A division of geological time that can be defined by the types of animals or plants that existed then. Typically a period lasts for tens of millions of years, and is further sub-divided into sub-periods, epochs, sub-epochs, and then stages.

Phenomenon A fact or situation that is observed to exist or happen, especially the existence of something which is in question.

Plankton The tiny animal and plant life that drifts in the waters of the ocean.

Plate tectonics The process whereby the surface of the Earth is continually being created and destroyed—new material being formed along ocean ridges and old material being lost down ocean trenches. The movement involved causes the continents to travel over the Earth's surface.

Plateau A flat area of high land.

Plesiosaur A large fossil marine reptile of the Mesozoic era, with large, paddle-like limbs, and a long flexible neck.

Pliosaur A plesiosaur with a short neck, large head, and massive toothed jaws.

Primitive A very early stage in the development of a species.

Prosauropod Late Triassic period ancestors of long-necked, plant-eating dinosaurs.

Pterosaur One of a group of flying reptiles from the Mesozoic. They flew with leathery wings supported by an elongated finger, *Pterodactylus* was a pterosaur.

Pulverise To crush something into powder.

Radioactivity The process in which an atom of a particular element breaks down to form another element. This process is accompanied by a release of energy which is the basis of nuclear power.

Reef A ridge on the seabed giving rise to shallow water. Most reefs are formed from the remains of living creatures.

Rift valley A steep-sided valley formed by subsidence of the Earth's surface between nearly parallel faults.

Rock A naturally formed substance that makes up the Earth. A typical rock will be made of several different types of mineral.

Sauropod An extremely large herbivorous dinosaur, characterized by a long neck, long tail, small head, and trunk-like legs.

Savannah A grassy plain in a hot country with few or no trees.

Scavenger An animal that feeds off food other animals have killed, or that humans have thrown away.

Sediment Matter carried by water or wind and deposited on the land surface or seabed.

Sedimentary A type of rock that has formed from sediment deposited by water or wind.

Seismic Of or relating to earthquakes or other vibrations of the Earth and its crust.

Shingle A mass of small rounded pebbles, especially on a seashore.

Silica A hard, unreactive, colorless compound which occurs as quartz, and as the principal constituent of sandstone and other rocks.

Stegosaur A herbivorous dinosaur with a double row of large bony plates along the back.

Stereoscope A device by which two photographs of the same object at slightly different angles are viewed together, creating an impression of depth.

Strata Layers or series of layers of rock.

Stratigraphy The aspect of geology that deals with the sequence of deposition of rocks, their structures and fossils, and interprets them to find out about conditions of former times.

Tectonics Large-scale processes affecting the structure of the Earth's crust.

Thermals Warm rising currents of air.

Theropod A bipedal carnivorous dinosaur with long jaws, three-toed hind legs, and small front legs with clawed hands.

Thyreophorans A group of dinosaurs that carried armor. They consisted of the plated stegosaurs, like *Stegosaurus*, and the armored ankylosaurs, like *Euoplocephalus*.

Tissue The living substance of a body. Tissue is made up of cells, and is the substance from which organs are built.

Trilobite A segmented arthropod, common in Palaeozoic seas.

Tsunami A long high sea wave caused by an earthquake or other disturbance.

Tyrannosaurid A type of dinosaur characterized by a broad, massive skull, a short, powerful neck, and reduced "arms" with only two digits.

Vertebrate An animal with a backbone.

Volcano A mountain or hill having a crater or vent through which lava, rock fragments, hot vapor and gas are or have been erupted from the Earth's crust.

Index

Picture Credits
t = top, b = bottom, c= centre, l = left, r = right. On pages which have many images, A is the image at the top, B is the next one down and so on.

Alamy: OBC tl, 1, 2-3 (Worldfoto), 6-7 (Worldfoto), 18-19 background (Blaine Harrington III), 24-25 (Tim Graham), 64-65 background (Pegaz), 81C left (Mervyn Rees). **Lisa Alderson:** 7C, 11C, 33C, 70E, 77A. **John Alston:** 13D, E. **Archaeological Services, Durham University:** 75C. **American Museum of Natural History:** 29B (Peter May), 39B. **Ardea:** OFC (Francois Gohier), 46-47 (Francois Gohier). **Leonello Calvetti:** 10-11, 15C, 16-17, 25c, 28-29, 34-35, 35C right, 42t, 43cl, 77E, 78tr, 78bl, 79tr, 81C right, 91B right, 85D, 86B, 92A, C, 93A, B. **Kenneth Carpenter, Ph.D:** 75D. **Comstock Images:** 21D right. **Corbis:** OBCtr, 8-9 background photography (W. Perry Conway), 36-37 (Ian Hodgson/ Reuters), 86C (Corbis Sygma/ Siemoneit Ronald), 87B (Sam Forencich/ Veer). **© Crown Copyright/MOD. Reproduced with the permission of the Controller of Her Majesty's Stationery Office:** 17C. **Frank DeNota:** 18-19, 20-21, 22-23, 23B, 24tl, 56-57, 67bl, 82cr, 87A, 90tl. **Jean Dixon:** 35D right. **DK Images:** 13B, 53D (Luciano Corbella). **FLPA:** 12-13 background (Yva Momatiuk/ John Eastcott/ Minden Pictures), 39C right (Winfried Wisniewski). **Faujas de Saint Fond, B. 1799. Histoire Naturelle de la Montagne de Saint Pierre de Maëstricht. Paris, 263 pp., 54 pls. Provided Mike Everhart, Oceans of Kansas Paleontology:** 51B. **Fossil Finds:** 35B. **Getty Images:** OBC tc (Image bank), 26-27 background (Stone), 44-45 background (Taxi), 48-49 (Science Faction), 67br (Image Bank), 93C (Taxi), 93E (Science faction). **Geoscience:** 71A, 71B, 71D, 71F, 71H. **Gondwana Studios:** 51D. **Roger Harris:** 43t, 89A. **Andrew Kerr:** 50-51, 54cr, 55tr, 58-59, 59C, 60-61, 62-63, 64-65, 65C right. **Michele Koons & Jennie Sturm:** 75B. **Illustration by Berislav Krzic:** 47C. **Simon Mendez:** OFC, OBCtl, OBC tc, OBC tr, OBCb, 1, 2-3, 4F, 4G, 5F, 6-7, 8-9, 9D, 12-13, 14-15, 26-27, 33C, 36-37, 37C right, 38-39, 40-41, 41C left, 42bl, 46-47, 52-53, 66tl, 67tl, 67tr, 70B, 70C, 70G, 70H right, 70J right, 76A, 76B, 76D, 88E, 89B, 91D right. **Museum of Utah:** 17B. **Natural History Museum, Oslo:** 21D left. **Natural History Museum London:** 5B, 7B left, 9B, 17D (De Agostini), 21B (John Holmes), 21C (John Holmes), 23C, 33B, 39C left, 41B, 45C, 45D (Anness Publishing), 49D, 53B, 57C (John Sibbeck), 59D (John Sibbeck), 61B, 65D right (Anness Publishing), 70F (Michael Long), 70I left, 70I right, 72tl, 72b, 73b, 74B, 75A (PlantObserver.com), 76C

(Anness Publishing), 77B (Audrey Atuchin), 77C (Anness Publishing), 78br, 80C left, 81B left (Michael Long), 81B centre left (De Agostini), 81D, 84A, 87C, 88B, 88D (Anness Publishing), 90A, 90B, 90C, 91D left, 92B, 92D, 92F, 92G, 93D (De Agostini). **NaturePL:** 11D (Dave Watts), 14-15 Background, 16-17 background (Nick Garbutt), 38-39 background (Jurgen Freund), 40-41 (Anup Shah), 50-51 background (Neil Lucas), 53C (Todd Pusser), 82bl (Jose B. Ruiz). **Naturhistorisches Museum:** 15B. **NHPA:** 28-29 Background (Stephen Dalton), 30-31 background (John Shaw), 32-33 (John Shaw). **Oxford City Museum:** 5D. **Oxford Scientific:** 5H (Daniel Cox), 45D (Thomas Haider), 47F (Richard Herrmann), 59E (Tui De Roy). **Peterborough Museum:** 47B. **Photolibrary.com/ Rubberball:** 37C left. **Rex Features/ Everett Collection:** 66cr (20thC Fox), 84B, 85C, 86F. **Paul Sereno:** 81A left. **Luis Rey:** 4C, 70D, 70K, 77D. **Science Photo Library:** 4A, 4E, 25br (Gustoimages), 49E, 51C (Chris Butler), 57D (Jim Zipp), 68tl (David A. Hardy), 69tl (D. Van Ravenswaay), 69bl (D. Van Ravenswaay), 69br (David Parker), 70tl (Jim Amos), 74 tl (Ge Astro Space), 76tl (Nasa), 76 background (Christian Darkin), 77 background (Christian Darkin), 78tl (Gail Jankus), 79tl (Adrian Thomas), 79br (Gustoimages), 80tl (Alfred Pasieka), 80A left (Martin Land), 82tl (David Aubrey), 85B (Sheila Terry), 86E (Victor Habbick Visions), 88A (Sinclair Stammers), 89C (Martin Land). **Science Faction.net:** 5A, 27C (Louie Psihoyos). **Adam Stuart Smith/ The Plesiosaur Directory www.plesiosauria.com:** 53E. **Stevebloom.com:** 56-57 background. **Superstock:** 41D left, 51E (Prisma), 54bl (Age footstock), 55bl (pixtal). **Franco Tempesta:** 4D, 44-45, 50-51 (net), 80B centre right, 80B far right, 83r. **Ticktock Media Archive:** 7A, 9A, 11A,B,D left, D right, 13A, 15A,D,E,F, 17A, 21A, 23A, 27A, 29A, 33A, 35A, 37A,B, 39A, 41A, 45A,B,E, 47A, 49A, 51A, 53A, 57A, 59A, 61A, 65A, 69cl, 80C right, 84D. **Chris Tomlin:** 70H left, 70J left, 80A right. **Ian Troth:** 49F. **Valley Anatomical Preparations Inc:** 90A right. **Wikipedia:** 59B, 65B, 73t, 84C, 86A, 92E.